On the remote East Kazakhstan steppe – the 'Polygon' – where the Soviets tested their nuclear bombs, the cemetery outside the village of Kainar is almost bigger than the village itself. Grave after grave bears the pictures of young men and women, victims of cancer or suicide, the twin killers of the 'Polygon'. One young woman called Orazken Malkarbay died at the age of 20. Her pretty, smiling face gazes down from the cold headstone. Inscribed beneath her picture, the words:

She did not reach her 21st Spring and left us suddenly.

Crying Forever.

Her Father.

'Suddenly' is a well-known Kazakh euphemism for suicide.

CRYING FOREVER
A NUCLEAR DIARY

CRYING FOREVER
A NUCLEAR DIARY

Struan Stevenson

DogEar Publications
c/o SCCO,
Abbey Business Centre,
83 Princes Street,
Edinburgh,
Scotland
EH2 2ER
First published 2006

A catalogue record for this volume is
available from the British Library
ISBN-10: 1-903700-16-7
ISBN-13: 978-1-903700-16-8

Typeset and Project Managed by Edmund O'Connor
07985 213435 / edmundcjoconnor@hotmail.com

Background on the author and contributors

Struan Stevenson is a Conservative Member of the European Parliament (MEP) for Scotland. He is Vice President of the ruling EPP-ED Group of 267 MEPs in the European Parliament. Since his election as an MEP in 1999, he has campaigned vigorously to bring recognition and help to the victims of Soviet nuclear tests in East Kazakhstan, visiting the area many times. This illustrated diary was written by Struan Stevenson and covers these visits and the campaigns he conducted in Europe.

On each occasion he was accompanied by Elena Kachkova, his Siberian interpreter and assistant, and on the last two visits by international TV celebrity and photographer – Kimberley Joseph.

Kimberley Joseph is an actress currently working in Hollywood. She appeared in 'Home & Away' and Gladiators in her native Australia, before landing a leading role in the final series of 'Cold Feet' and in the US blockbuster series 'Lost'. Kimberley took many of the photographs which appear in this publication. Elena Kachkova is an interpreter and researcher. She was born and educated in the Soviet Union. Her parents were rocket scientists working in the closed city of Novosibirsk in Siberia. Elena served as a Captain in the Soviet military during her compulsory army training, before moving to the West. She now lives in South Africa.

Acknowledgements

I would like to thank my wife Pat and my sons Ryan and Gregor for their endless encouragement and patience. Their commitment and support enables me to dedicate time and effort to working for the people of Semipalatinsk in Kazakhstan.

My trusted team, with Luisa Strani and Lisa Rose in my office in Brussels and Belinda Don in Edinburgh, provides me with the structure and enthusiasm to support my work. My PR team, Elaine McKean and Jacqui Low at Indigo, have offered professional advice and dedication to publicise this illustrated diary.

None of this would be possible without the financial backing of our sponsors who have shown their commitment by supporting the international exhibition of photos, namely the EPP-ED group in the European Parliament, Unilever, Diageo, One World Design, Lloyds TSB, Nike, Royal Mail, Scottish & Newcastle and the Republic of Kazakhstan. A number of individuals, who have asked for their contributions to remain anonymous, have also ensured that this project has successfully raised the profile of the plight of the people of East Kazakhstan, the real victims of the Cold War.

I am grateful to each and every one of the people who have put their faith in me not to become simply *"another disaster tourist"*. I promise to continue my association with Kazakhstan until I am no longer needed.

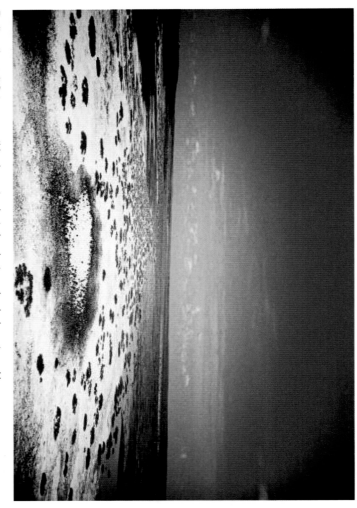

Radioactive salt flats – everything is contaminated – plants, animals, insects and humans

Introduction

From 1949 until 1990, the Soviet Union used the Semipalatinsk region of East Kazakhstan as a nuclear testing site. Hidden from the world, this top-secret site the size of Wales was subjected to 607 nuclear explosions, including 26 above ground tests, 124 atmospheric tests and 457 underground. Cynically, the military scientists would wait until the wind was blowing in the direction of the remote Kazakh villages before detonating their nuclear devices. KGB doctors would then closely study the effects of nuclear radiation on their own population.

After widespread protests by the Kazakh population, President Gorbachev ordered a moratorium on all further tests in 1990. When the Soviet Union collapsed in December 1991, the departing battalions of troops and secret police, who had guarded the 'Polygon' left a legacy of devastation and sickness. The 1.5 million population of the Polygon were subjected to the equivalent of 20,000 Hiroshima bombs. Seepage from the underground tests has polluted watercourses and streams. Farmland has been heavily irradiated. Radioactive contamination has entered the food chain.

Now cancers run at five times the national average. Cancers of the throat, lungs and breasts are particularly common. Twelve year old girls have developed breast cancer. Birth defects are three times the national average. Babies and farm animals are born with terrible deformities. Children are mentally retarded and Downs Syndrome is common. Virtually all children suffer from anaemia. Many of the young men are impotent. Many of the young women are afraid to become pregnant in case they give birth to defective babies.

Psychological disorders are rife. Suicides are widespread, especially among young men and even, alarmingly among children. Fourteen children and teenagers committed suicide in Karaul village alone during 2004, including an eleven-year-old boy and a twelve-year-old girl. Average life expectancy is 52, compared to 59 outside the Polygon.

Contents

Map of Kazakhstan

2000 – Ground Zero

Monday 21st August 2000 – Kazakh National Academy of Science, Almaty

"The first indication we had that nuclear bombs were being detonated was in 1957. A doctor friend of mine from Semipalatinsk said that he had noticed strange discoloured lesions on the skin of some of his patients. He knew I had been involved in investigations following Hiroshima and Nagasaki and asked me to have a look. I confirmed that these were radiation burns."

Professor Saim Balmukhanov slammed his fist on the table. *"People in the West cannot begin to understand what we suffered in the name of Socialism. One and a half million people in Kazakhstan were exposed to high radiation doses during the Soviet nuclear testing programme. But when I reported my findings to Moscow they denied it. For more than forty years they claimed that the high incidence of cancers and babies born with genetic deformities, were hereditary diseases caused by the poor Kazakh diet."*

Professor Balmukhanov is 78 years old but looks much younger. He still works in the Kazakh National Academy of Science in Almaty, where he was first appointed Professor and Head of Department in 1946 at the age of only 24. He is still Head of the Department of Biology and Medicine. His eyes sparkle as he speaks. He has made it his life's work to uncover the horrible legacy bequeathed to his people by the Soviet Empire. Twice, this much-decorated war hero was arrested and stripped of his Communist Party membership when his enquiries got too close to the truth.

He recounted how between 1949 and 1990, the Soviet military exploded a total of 607 nuclear bombs in a massive, top-secret test site near the remote, eastern Kazakh town of Semipalatinsk, on the Siberian border. Of course there had been rumours of explosions and strange mushroom clouds and village houses being swept away in the aftershock of the blasts. But people were afraid to speak out. The whole area around Semipalatinsk, equal to the size of Wales, was closed and strictly controlled by the military. Villagers were told that they should be proud to be part of the great technological advances of the Soviet Union.

"There were sudden deaths and miscarriages," the Professor said *"but each time we challenged Moscow they lied to us. When we checked the health of villagers within the Polygon – the 18,500 sq km territory of the core test site – against that of villagers from outside, we discovered there were four-times fewer diseases outside the Polygon. Finally in 1958 the Soviet military authorities had to admit responsibility."*

Professor Balmukhanov spread several large ledgers on the table of his study. Each was prominently marked 'Top Secret' in Russian. *"These are the Soviet records of the human impact caused by their nuclear tests. The KGB right from the outset carefully recorded every piece of medical evidence. But all of it was highly classified and kept locked in a Moscow vault. Information, which could have helped us to treat patients and save lives, was withheld for 40 years. Only when the Soviet Empire collapsed in 1992 did we finally gain access to this material. Even now, the Russians are still holding on to a lot of information."*

This was to be the first of many encounters with Professor Saim Balmukhanov. It is a tradition in Kazakhstan that when people become close friends they form a 'family'. Professor Balmukhanov now regards me as his 'son' and I look up to him as my wise and erudite 'father.' I visit my 'father' and his family every time I go to Kazakhstan. This first meeting with him in Almaty in August 2000 came about almost by chance. It had been brokered at an earlier encounter in Brussels, shortly after my election as a Member of the European Parliament, in 1999.

Late in the afternoon during one hot, damp, September in 1999, I was telephoned in my office in the European Parliament in Brussels by a friend and former Green MEP from Germany, Frank Schwalba-Hoth. Frank asked if I had a few moments to spare as he wanted me to meet a doctor from Kazakhstan. I protested that I was too busy but when Frank persisted, I finally caved in and agreed, insisting that the meeting should last no more than fifteen minutes. It was to be fifteen minutes that changed my life!

Frank introduced me to Dr Kamila Magzieva, a scientific consultant and a strikingly beautiful woman aged forty-something, with jet black hair and typical Kazakh features. As she described to me the plight of the people of Semipalatinsk in East Kazakhstan and told me of the 607 nuclear bombs that had been detonated there and how the Soviets had treated the local Kazakh population as human guinea pigs, I was both fascinated and horrified.

I told Kamila that everyone in the West had, of course, heard of the enormous tragedy of Chernobyl, partly because the fallout had affected the West. But Chernobyl was a single nuclear explosion – an accident. I had never heard of the hundreds of nuclear explosions in Semipalatinsk. This was almost unbelievable. I asked Kamila if I could come to Kazakhstan and see the evidence for myself. She was overjoyed.

She told me later that her meeting with me was the ninth she had held that day, which was the 9th of September 1999. Kamila thought that there was some sort of karma at work on 9-9-99. Of her nine meetings in the European Parliament, I was the MEP who agreed to follow up her request to help her beleaguered people.

So it was in August 2000 that I found myself undertaking the first of many visits to Kazakhstan with Elena Kachkova, my vivacious and sometimes outrageous Russian interpreter. Elena was born and educated in Siberia. She rose to the rank of Captain in the Soviet army during her compulsory military service. She is a total professional, who can match the hard drinking Kazakhs toast for toast at an official dinner without missing a beat of her flawless interpretation. Our trips to Kazakhstan would involve me in a campaign to draw attention to these victims of the Cold War and their appalling suffering and would embrace me in a new Kazakh 'family' with Kamila as my 'sister' and Professor Saim Balmukhanov as my 'father.'

Tuesday 22nd August 2000 – The Polygon, East Kazakhstan

The village of Znamenka lies in the heart of the Polygon. It was one of the worst affected villages. It is a typical ramshackle, Kazakh affair, with mud-bricked and grass-roofed huts, baking in plus 40 degrees centigrade in summer and shivering in minus 40 degrees in the snowbound winter of the steppes. This would be an unwelcoming place to live at the best of times. But now is the worst of times. The departure of the Soviets in 1992 led to economic collapse. An attempt by the Kazakh authorities to privatise the old system of collective farming failed. There is high unemployment and no job opportunities. There is also the legacy of the Cold War.

The village elders tell their story to anyone who dares to visit. Unlike their Russian speaking neighbours from the city, they still speak Kazakh. Many remember the ground shaking beneath their feet and the mushroom clouds rising in the distance. They were encouraged to come out of their homes to watch. The authorities told them they were privileged to witness the might of the Soviet military machine. They were not told that many bombs were detonated only when strong winds could ensure a thick cloud of radioactive dust would blow in their direction.

Now cancers run at five times the national average. Cancers of the throat, lungs and breasts are particularly common. Twelve year old girls have developed breast cancer. Birth defects are three times the national average. Babies and farm animals are born with terrible deformities. Many of the young men are impotent. Many of the young women are afraid to become pregnant in case they give birth to defective babies. Psychological disorders are rife. Suicides are widespread, especially amongst young men. Average life expectancy is 52, compared to 59 outside the Polygon.

The women of Znamenka had gathered in the school to await the arrival of our party. I was accompanied by Elena, Kamila,

Elderly women of Znamenka with staff from the village clinic

20

the Akim (Mayor) of Semipalatinsk and the Minister of Education from the Kazakh Government and various other civil servants. The school is the only three-storey building in the village. Built in Soviet times, it caters for more than 500 children.

The Head Teacher told us that their entire budget for the whole of the previous year amounted to $160. Even so, the villagers had somehow managed to paint the classrooms and hall. I offered the Head Teacher some children's educational DVDs from the European Parliament and immediately felt silly, when he declined and explained that the school had no electricity. I made him take the DVDs nevertheless and told the Minister of Education that I would return next year and expected the school to have been supplied with electricity and the kids to have seen the DVDs.

Fifty or sixty local women had gathered in the main hall of the school. They had come to tell their stories to the foreign visitors. They explained that everything is contaminated – plants, animals, insects and humans. Radiation and salt have polluted their only source of water. They are forced to eat the few sickly cows and sheep that remain. Nearly every woman in the room was visibly ill.

A 38 year old said her breast was removed last year due to cancer, but she was lucky to have found a job and must work to live as her husband had died of cancer. She looked pale and sick. An old lady was helped to her feet. She explained that her joints are stiff and crippled – a common ailment in the Polygon. She was sure it was due to the radiation. Her husband died of cancer two years ago. She can't walk and can't work and has

Dental equipment abandoned by the Soviets still in use in Semipalatinsk

no one to turn to for help. Despite her appearance she was only 48 years old. Premature ageing is another common feature. The tears rolled down her cheeks as her friends helped her back to her seat. A big lady in a tattered dress summed up the mood of the meeting. *"All we need is clothes to wear and food to eat to be like anyone else in the world."*

Across the street in the village medical centre the local doctor and nurses were struggling to cope. Often these dedicated people go without pay for weeks. There is little money for basic medicines and no money for equipment. They have to deal with all the usual medical problems of a remote rural community numbering 4,000 people but, in addition, they have the cancers, birth defects and illnesses caused by the nuclear tests. They work in a ramshackle shed with a tin roof. An old broken fridge acts as a medicine cabinet.

The doctor explained that she has 70 patients whose medical conditions are directly attributable to the nuclear legacy. However, the State authorities demand a rigorous series of tests over many months, and sometimes years, before they will provide a certificate accepting the patient as a radiation victim. Such certificates entitle the victims to a tiny weekly payment and free medicines.

An elderly mother brought her son into the room. Like many of his peers he had severe learning difficulties. He was 21 but had the mind of a four year old. He suffered from epileptic convulsions and years ago the local doctor prescribed a specific drug she knew would help. The mother wept as she described her frustration. She waved the old, crumpled prescription in her hand. The authorities had still not classified her son as a victim of the bomb tests and she could no longer afford to pay for his medicine. The doctor said that only seven out of the 70 local radiation victims had been classified.

I had prepared some envelopes containing $10, $20 and $50 US dollars. I handed the doctor a $50 envelope and the elderly mother a $20. They looked mystified. The Akim (Mayor) of Semipalatinsk saw what I was doing and whispered to me that it was impossible to fund a relief operation for the entire Polygon out of my own pocket.

When we left the crumbling clinic, we could see a small group of village elders – all men – had gathered on the opposite side of the dusty track awaiting our arrival. The elders looked extremely stern. One old and wrinkled man with a brightly embroidered cap and two glistening, gold-filled front teeth, drew himself up to his full height and launched into a short lecture. *"We get frequent visitors from the West"* he said. *"Politicians who come to gape and stare and promise to help, but are never heard from again. We hope that you are not one of these 'disaster tourists' "* he ended. At that point there was a sudden noise of running feet across the street. We all turned to look and were astonished to see the doctor in her billowing white coat, running towards us, leaving a cloud of dust in her wake. She was waving the $50 I had just given her and which she had obviously just uncovered from the sealed envelope. She jabbered excitedly in Kazakh to the elders, who quickly lightened up and one by one, started hugging and kissing me on each cheek.

It was this encounter with these dignified and wise village elders of Znamenka which more than anything else made me determined not to become a 'disaster tourist', but to provide some tangible help to these beleaguered people.

Wednesday 23rd August 2000 – Kurchatov

Driving out of Semipalatinsk over the cracked and pot-holed road, the crumbling ruins of the Cold War soon become apparent. The road to Ground Zero, where the nuclear weapons were detonated, stretches for hundreds of kilometres across the barren steppe. During the Soviet era, massive security surrounded the Polygon. Whole cities were erected to house military and scientific personnel. Their names never appeared on any maps. Residents were forbidden to mention where they lived, even to a neighbour from a nearby village.

About 80 kilometres from Semipalatinsk is Chagan, built between 1947 and 1949 as a base for the Soviet army and airforce, the city is now completely deserted and derelict. Street after street of broken tenements bears silent witness to the nuclear arms race. Weeds sprout from cracks between crazily rearing flagstones. A statue of Lenin tilts dangerously to the side, the nose broken off and the base scrawled with graffiti. In the crumbling foyer of the cinema, a huge reel spews strips of brittle film onto the cracked floor tiles. I picked up a small section and held it up to the light. I was staring at frames from 'The Battleship Potemkin'. The silence of this deserted city was only broken by the noise of birds singing in the bushes sprouting from the long-neglected flowerbeds.

Beyond Chagan the tarmac road occasionally gives way to a muddy dirt track. There is no money for repairs. This remote and arid steppe, across which Ghengis Khan marched his vast army, was once the haunt of nomadic farmers. But in 1947,

Elena beside one of the monitoring towers built by the Soviets to measure the effects of nuclear detonations

that all changed. The territory was chosen by the Soviet Defence Ministry as their nuclear test site. Tens of thousands of workers poured into the area, which was quickly transformed into one of the richest parts of the Soviet Empire. By 1949 the huge construction programme was complete. Roads, railways, water supply conduits, power and communication lines, towns and cities were built to a high technical standard. A sophisticated infrastructure was put in place to measure the atomic blasts around Ground Zero.

It was at the end of the line on the Trans-Siberian Railway in 1946 that Josef Stalin ordered a new town to be built. On the remote plains of Kazakhstan, the USSR's leading physicists began to assemble. Their top-secret task was to build Stalin an atomic bomb. Three years later, Kurchatov – the town named after the nuclear scientist who led the project – fulfilled its promise to Stalin.

At 7:00 am on August 29th, 1949, near the village of Dolon, the Soviet Union detonated its first atomic bomb. It was the first of 607 nuclear devices secretly exploded at Ground Zero over the next four decades. The city of Kurchatov, 150 kilometres from Semipalatinsk, was home to over 30,000 residents, including scientists such as Andrei Sakharov and Stalin's notorious KGB Chief, Lavrenty Beria. Stalin had ordered Beria to execute Sakharov and Kurchatov if the first atomic test had failed.

Further massive above ground explosions in 1951 and the first plutonium bomb in 1953 followed. A colossal thermo-nuclear device was dropped onto the site from an aircraft in 1955, sending a radioactive cloud across most of Kazakhstan and into China. Only sustained protests and peace marches by the courageous Kazakh people, largely ignored in the West, finally forced the Soviets to abandon plans for further tests in 1990.

Now only 9,000 people live in Kurchatov City. Most of the scientists who remain are engaged in the study of radiation and nuclear safety. There is mass unemployment and a tangible air of despondency. Like elsewhere in the Polygon, the city is crumbling.

It was the elderly Professor Balmukhanov who told me why Kurchatov had come to be knows as 'The City of Angels' during the Soviet era. A little peasant village belonging to a poor Soviet collective farm (sovkhoz), called Kzyl-Zhuldys (The Red Star), nestled against a steep bank of the River Irtysh deep inside the Polygon, near Kurchatov. There were only 30 to 40 houses here in the 1950's, but the whole village was more than a kilometre long. Each house was surrounded by a large cattle yard with rudimentary, corrugated tin byres.

One evening, everybody was waiting anxiously for the old cowhand to come back from the pastures with the village cows. The women of Kzyl-Zhuldys were waiting to milk their cows and use the milk to boil a fistful of barley, or, for the luckier ones, some wheat, providing lunch and dinner combined for the whole family. But there was no sign of the cows or of their elderly keeper who was called Aktykoz. The women were becoming increasingly grumpy, cursing Aktykoz while others tried to calm them down, reasoning that he'd probably taken the cows to farther pastures where there was better grass. Suddenly, they heard the cows. The herd had found its own way home, but there was no sign of Aktykoz.

The roads in rural Kazakhstan are often poorly-maintained or little more than dirt tracks

29

A search party was sent out into the steppe to look for him, but to no avail. He had disappeared. It was some weeks later before he returned with his strange tale and the legend of the 'City of Angels' took root.

Apparently Aktykoz had been tending to his herd of cows when he was spotted by a mobile military unit from Kurchatov, whose job it was to protect the top secret nuclear test site in the Polygon. They regarded the old cowhand as a suspicious person. He was arrested and taken to Kurchatov. While checks were made on his identity, he was held in the military jail. However, young soldiers, conscripted from nearby villages, felt sorry for the old man. They gave him extra food and never locked him up for the night like a criminal. One night Aktykoz took advantage of his situation. Escaping from his cell he crept along darkened streets until he reached the city limits. As dawn broke, he recognised an old cemetery two or three kilometres away from the nearest military check-point and decided to hide there. When he approached it, however, he found to his surprise that the cemetery had been desecrated and all of the graves had been removed and replaced by a makeshift army barracks.

Soon, he was picked up by a patrol and taken back to Kurchatov jail. However, the conscripts decided not to report him to their commandant. They were fond of the old man and admired his bravery in trying to escape. He asked them what had happened to the old cemetery. Where had all the bodies gone? They told him that his temporary hiding place was all that remained of an old barracks built by political prisoners brought from all over the country to construct the Polygon nuclear site. The prisoners were then taken away and rumour had it that they were shot and buried inside tunnels blasted into a nearby mountain range.

"But, where has the cemetery gone?" – asked Aktykoz.

"There no longer is one" – came the reply.

"And where do you bury your dead people?"

"Nobody dies here, and those who reach 50 just fly away."

"They fly away? But where?"

This question from Aktykoz was met by silence from the soldiers, some of whom glanced upwards, towards the sky.

It was only years later that the truth about the 'City of Angels' leaked out. Indeed it was true that Kurchatov did not have a cemetery, and nobody was buried there, on the orders of a paranoid Stalin. The ill and the dying were taken to a city in Ukraine, called Yellow Waters, where they were buried in a cemetery protected and patrolled by the KGB.

In 1989 Professor Balmukhanov questioned Colonel Turapin of the KGB about the real reasons why there was no cemetery in Kurchatov. He said it was not much of a secret. The bones and teeth of the dead retain plutonium and, if properly measured, it is possible to get an accurate idea about the size and strength of the nuclear devices which had been detonated in the area. Colonel Turapin said that there were always fears about possible spies trying to dig up the dead, so Stalin ordered that no-one should ever again be buried in Kurchatov.

Thursday 24th August 2000 – Ground Zero

As you leave Kurchatov, a few kilometres on from the last former Soviet army checkpoint, the tarmac ends and the journey to Ground Zero continues off-road, across the parched and endless steppe. Despite the searing heat, vehicle windows have to be kept tightly shut to avoid inhaling plutonium particles in the swirling clouds of dust. Elena, Kamila and I were packed inside an old minibus perspiring in the sweltering heat. A young scientist – complete with Geiger Counter – a press photographer and a driver made up our small party. Soon, a spiral of dust could be seen approaching fast across the steppe. It was a local villager riding an old motorcycle/sidecar combination, hurrying to escape arrest for pilfering copper wire and metal from Ground Zero.

The Kazakhs do not have the resources to police the test site and despite the fact that spending more than ten minutes at the epicentre is lethally dangerous, many villagers camp on the site for days, digging up the hundreds of kilometres of copper wire used to detonate the bombs. They know they will die in a few years from radiation poisoning. But they say they will die anyway from starvation. At least, they argue, this way they earn enough to feed their families, by selling the copper across the border to the Chinese. The problem is, this deadly radioactive copper is then fashioned into jewellery and sold in China or exported to the West.

At five kilometres from Ground Zero the first series of reinforced concrete towers, still bearing nuclear blast monitoring equipment, can be seen. Nearer Ground Zero, the towers are little more than mangled heaps of steel and

A nuclear crater in the heart of the Polygon

concrete. Rocks and stones have been turned to glass. The eerie stillness of the place belies its former hideous purpose.

Here sheep, pigs, cattle and dogs were tethered to stakes to await the scorching nuclear blast. A whole small, uninhabited town was erected nearby with two shops, a metro station, a factory and road and railway bridges, all to see what impact a nuclear blast would have on a typical settlement. Scarecrows dressed as soldiers were dotted around. Military machinery, artillery pieces, tanks, aeroplanes, transport vehicles and armoured cars were placed at different distances around the epicentre to study the impact of the bomb. Now the tangled detritus is all that remains. The shrill bleeping of a Geiger Counter broke the silence. A lizard rustled in the undergrowth around the rim of the massive crater. Locusts hopped aimlessly from plant to plant. The ground shimmered in the heat.

The young scientist looked at his watch. *"You've been here for more than ten minutes already"* he said. *"We must go."* The photographer was still taking pictures of the crater. We shouted to him to hurry. We were all being exposed to dangerously high levels of radiation.

Hours later, back in Kurchatov, we were told to throw away our shoes and clothes and to wash thoroughly in a shower. This was easier said than done. The one available shower managed barely a trickle of water. *"Drink plenty of vodka"* our friendly scientist advised. *"It flushes the radiation out of your system. If you don't, you will feel really ill tomorrow."* We took his advice and drank lots of local Kazakh vodka and still felt really ill the next day!

Friday 25th August 2000 – The Andas-Altyn Gold Mine

One hundred kilometres away from Kurchatov was a vision of the future. The Andas-Altyn Mining Company, a Scottish-Canadian-Kazakh operation, which opened a gold mine in January 2000. Already by August they were employing 530 Kazakhs and paying good wages. They told us they had mined almost one tonne of gold in the past six months.

The dynamic Mayor of Semipalatinsk, Nurlan Omarov, said he was keen to see further inward investment to his region. He knows that the road to salvation for Semipalatinsk will rely as much on the efforts of his own people to help themselves as on foreign aid.

Even at this distance from the test sites, the workers were still being exposed to dangerously high levels of radiation. Underground nuclear tests contaminated the rock strata and penetrated the water courses. But at least these miners have a job. For tens of thousands of innocent, unemployed Kazakhs, the legacy of the Cold War is one of suffering and hardship. There is little inward investment. Few have the courage to build a business in a former nuclear test site.

2001 – Beyond Chernobyl

On my return to Europe from Kazakhstan I was deeply troubled. I remembered the village elders in Znamenka who had sternly warned me how 'disaster tourists' offer to help, but are rarely heard of again. I had given these dignified people a solemn pledge that I would help and now I was concerned about how such assistance could, realistically, be provided.

I spoke to some colleagues who have expertise in the EU budget and asked how best I could channel some much-needed funding to the people of Semipalatinsk and the Polygon. They advised me to apply to the Tacis Programme. Launched by the European Commission in 1991, the Tacis Programme provides grant-financed technical assistance to twelve countries of Eastern Europe and Central Asia (Armenia, Azerbaijan, Belarus, Georgia, Kazakhstan, Kyrgyzstan, Moldova, Russia, Tajikistan, Turkmenistan, Ukraine and Uzbekistan), and was mainly aimed at enhancing the transition process in these countries.

However, adding new lines to the EU budget is never an easy process. The experts advised me to look for an existing budget line to which I could add a fairly innocuous amendment. This, they assured me, would have a much greater chance of success.

After many hours of scouring through page after page of budget items I finally struck gold. Under the heading 'Funding for the victims of Chernobyl', I discovered a budget line of €10 million. By submitting a simple amendment which sought to change the heading from 'Funding for the victims of Chernobyl' to 'Funding for the victims of radiation', I could open the door to some significant aid.

Angry village elders in Sarzhal

I tabled my amendment with an accompanying explanatory statement which outlined the plight of the people of Semipalatinsk and the need for up to €4 million of Tacis aid to be directed to the Polygon in East Kazakhstan. Sure enough, when the budget was voted through Committee in September 2001 and then adopted by the full plenary session of the European Parliament in Strasbourg in October, this minor amendment slipped through unscathed. I had won my first major battle. €4 million was now guaranteed.

Now I had to begin the work of raising the profile of these Cold War victims in the West. Most people I spoke to about Semipalatinsk reacted like I had done when I first heard about the Soviet nuclear tests. A combination of shock and horror, coupled with astonishment that they had never come across this issue before. It was evident that a major publicity campaign was going to be necessary just to highlight the suffering of these people before I could hope to mobilise any sympathy or financial aid.

I concluded that it is wrong for the West to sit back and ignore the plight of the people of Semipalatinsk. These are the real victims of the Cold War and the Cold War involved the West. The Soviet Union waged nuclear war on its own people and now they need our help. The EU has given unstinting financial aid to the victims of the Chernobyl nuclear accident. Although it was an appalling tragedy, it nevertheless represented a single nuclear explosion. The people of Semipalatinsk have to live with the horrific legacy of 607 nuclear explosions.

Kazakhstan is set to be a major oil exporter, with oil reserves similar to those of Saudi Arabia. As a nation it will therefore be an invaluable strategic partner for the EU in Central Asia. It is, nevertheless, struggling to rebuild the shattered post-Soviet economy, utilising the inward investment that is already attracted to the country by the oil industry. Although Kazakhstan is one of the strongest economic performers in the region, it will be at least another ten years before there are sufficient financial resources to enable tangible assistance to be given to the victims of radiation in Semipalatinsk. It was my belief that there was therefore an urgent need for interim aid at least in the short-term.

I decided that it was necessary to target aid from the West towards three main areas:

- The purchase of medical equipment for oncology units in regional hospitals in Semipalatinsk and the surrounding territory;
- Medical programmes to assist cancer sufferers in the Polygon; and
- Emergency aid for villages and rural dwellers affected by radiation in the Polygon.

In order to kick-start the process of securing EU aid for Semipalatinsk, it was necessary for me to raise the profile of the Soviet nuclear testing legacy. Everyone in the West has heard of Chernobyl, but few have heard of Semipalatinsk. I therefore set about arranging a series of events aimed at addressing this lack of information.

To begin with I organised a visit, to the European Parliament in Strasbourg, of a high-level delegation from Kazakhstan, led by the Deputy Foreign Minister Mr Kairat Abousseitov. This was followed in late February 2001 by a highly successful seminar and photo exhibition on Semipalatinsk, held in the European Parliament in Brussels. Around 50 MEPs and parliamentary staff attended the seminar to hear the Foreign Minister, Mr Erlan Idrissov, and a number of eminent politicians and clinicians from Semipalatinsk, give graphic accounts of the post-Soviet nuclear legacy.

In addition, over 100 people, including many MEPs, attended a reception in the Parliament to open the exhibition of photographs of the victims of the Soviet nuclear testing programme.

Based on the success of this venture in Brussels, I arranged for the exhibition and seminar to travel to Scotland, where we again staged a reception and discussion on Semipalatinsk in the new Scottish Parliament in Edinburgh. The Kazakh Ambassador to the UK, Ambassador Akhmetov, was able to meet with the Presiding Officer of the Scottish Parliament, Sir David Steel, and many other prominent Members of the Scottish Parliament. The subsequent seminar, attended by a number of parliamentarians, parliamentary staff, leading charity workers and journalists, was chaired by the Deputy Presiding Officer George Reid. The exhibition of photographs then travelled to Ireland, first to Dublin, then in November 2001, to Cork.

All of this activity created interest in the media and I wrote several feature articles for key UK and foreign newspapers. But of course, raising the profile of the Soviet nuclear testing legacy was only half the battle. The main objective was to secure aid. Apart from the €4 million in the EU's Tacis fund, I wanted something tangible to take to the villagers in the Polygon when I next returned.

Through some contacts in the European Parliament I approached Nike the international sports goods manufacturer. They were happy to help. Although Nike has no commercial interests in Kazakhstan whatsoever, they agreed to supply me with crates of sweatshirts and baseball caps and with $5,000 cash to hand out to the villagers in the Polygon.

2002 – The Soviet Legacy

In 2002, I returned to Kazakhstan to speak at the 'Drive For A World Without Nuclear Arms' conference in Almaty, where President Nazarbayev of Kazakhstan and Mikhail Gorbachev were also VIP guests. Ironically Gorbachev, the former Soviet President, is now an environmental campaigner trying to repair some of the damage done by the Soviet regime. It was Gorbachev who finally put an end to the testing in Kazakhstan after an uprising in 1990. The site near Semipalatinsk was shut down for good in 1991.

I had an interesting meeting with Gorbachev, although Elena shook like a leaf throughout. To Elena, thinking back to her days in the Soviet military, Gorbachev had been the all-powerful emperor and it was astonishing to see this confident, assertive woman visibly shaking as she sat between her former President and me, acting as interpreter.

We discussed what was going on in Semipalatinsk and how the European Parliament could help. Gorbachev asked, *"Where is all the money going? I keep hearing about all these huge amounts they are spending in Europe, like giving a billion euros to tobacco farmers and yet to try and find some assistance for the beleaguered citizens of Kazakhstan is so hard."*

Gorbachev said I could use his name and tell everybody he would support trying to find emergency aid for these people. While Gorbachev himself authorised some of the tests at Ground Zero, the former Soviet leader deserves credit for ending the Cold War. Gorbachev was the one who came up with the initiative at summits in Geneva and Reykjavik in the 1980s. He suggested a nuclear non-proliferation treaty and the

Americans were taken aback. It was his initiative to start winding down the whole arms race. He told me that when the people rose up in Kazakhstan against nuclear testing, it helped to lead towards the collapse of the Soviet Union. He admitted all that. He came across as a man of great sincerity to me.

There is still pressure from some of the Russian scientists who protest that nothing was wrong and they were only matching what America was doing. They said in the Cold War, it took two to tango. But Gorbachev is now very much on the side of the angels. He has set up the Gorbachev Foundation and his objective is to redress the balance, to put right the environmental damage caused by the Soviet Union.

At the conference, Gorbachev was given a standing ovation and treated as a hero. But during the session I was chairing, there was a Soviet nuclear scientist who defended the tests and was barracked and shouted at by many of the Kazakhs. People were asking why the West is so ignorant of the suffering they have had to endure. *"Why does the West know everything about Chernobyl and nothing about Semipalatinsk?"* they were shouting. I replied that it's partly because Chernobyl affected us in the West while Semipalatinsk didn't affect us directly. But, I said it was obvious that as a fledgling independent economy, Kazakhstan cannot afford even the most basic medical equipment or supplies for its people in the former test zone. And the Kazakhs are still fighting to have top secret KGB medical records released by Moscow.

I was also disturbed to learn that conditions could worsen with the impending closure of a vital hospital in the area. I received an emotionally-charged phone call from the chief doctor in

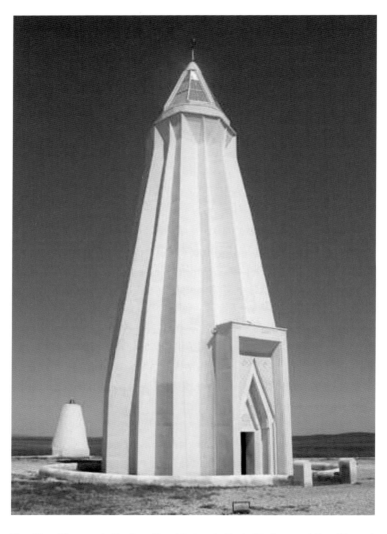

The Abay Museum in Eastern Kazakhstan dedicated to the great Kazakh poet and humanitarian Abay Kunanbaev

Kurchatov Hospital. She was in floods of tears as she explained in broken English how the authorities had told her the hospital was to be closed for economic reasons. I went on state television to plead with President Nazarbayev to postpone the closure. I said on TV *"I have lodged an amendment to the European Parliament's annual budget. I have asked for €4 million from the Tacis fund to help Kazakhstan. I would hope that some of the money can go towards stopping the closure of the hospital."* I explained that the 50-bed hospital at Kurchatov, the town Stalin built to house the nuclear scientists, is needed now more than ever.

The extremes of temperature in summer and winter and harsh weather conditions, have mostly destroyed the roads across the steppe. It is virtually impossible for people living in the remote Kazakh villages to access medical assistance. *"They cannot be expected to travel hundreds of miles to hospital in Semipalatinsk City. It is essential that their local hospital in Kurchatov is saved"* I said. Later I heard that my plea had been successful and the hospital was both retained and modernised with financial aid from the Kazakh government.

I also told the TV interviewers, *"I have talked to some of the leading academics from the State Medical Academy who told me that the genetic effects of radiation exposure have multiplied down the generations. They say future generations will suffer even worse cancers and deformities. Gorbachev said in his speech that the land around this enormous area of the Polygon will not be fit for agriculture for 300 years. Yet if the people of Semipalatinsk hadn't risen up and marched through the barbed wire, the testing wouldn't have stopped."*

2003 – Tears in the Polygon

Back in Scotland, I set about organising my next visit to the Polygon. A journalist and a photographer from a leading Scottish Sunday newspaper were keen to accompany me. I cleared their trip with the Kazakh Embassy in London and visas were issued well in advance.

However, with only days to go before our departure, the editor telephoned me to tell me that a major problem had arisen. The newspaper's insurers were refusing to cover the reporter and photographer, because of the perceived dangers of visiting the Polygon. The two men in question were devastated. They really wanted to come, but the editor had withdrawn funding for the trip. He could not afford to risk the potential of a massive claim against his newspaper, should either of the men develop cancer or some other serious illness through exposure to radiation in Kazakhstan.

This only served to remind me of the appalling conditions the population of Semipalatinsk are forced to live day by day.

Tuesday 5th August 2003 – Almaty

After a KLM flight from the UK to Almaty via Amsterdam, Kimberley, Elena and I arrived at 2.00am in the searing heat of the old airport, devoid of air conditioning, and took our place in long queues while Kazakh officials laboriously checked hundreds of visas. Dr Kamila Magzieva, my great friend and Kazakh 'sister', arrived and rescued us by demanding that we be taken through a priority channel because we were carrying aid goods for the people of Semipalatinsk. It took six airport trolleys to carry all the enormous cartons of sweatshirts and caps generously donated by NIKE and transported free of charge by KLM. Outside in the airport car park, dozens of boys vied for the job of carrying our baggage, in exchange for a few tenge ($1 = 140 tenge).

After a short sleep and a shower we met Danabek Jusup of BBC Central Asia & Caucasus Service, who was to stay with us for our entire visit. We headed for a meeting with Andrew Dinsley, Deputy Ambassador in the British Embassy. He informed us that the British Government had just commenced a consultancy project to establish which areas of the Polygon were safe for grazing. He agreed that Kazakhstan is set to become the richest country in Central Asia as it develops its huge oil reserves, but noted that little of this windfall has found its way to the beleaguered people of the Polygon.

Later we met Alan Waddams, the EU Ambassador to Kazakhstan, and discussed the €4 million Tacis fund for Semipalatinsk, which I successfully lobbied for in the 2001 European Parliament's budget. I complained that much of this money seems to end up in the pockets of Western consultants, saying *"You could now cover the Polygon with paper from their reports"*. We resolved that both the Kazakh Prime Minister and I should write to European Commissioner Chris Patten asking for at least half of this fund to be spent on a new breast cancer centre in the hospital in Semipalatinsk.

Wednesday 6th August 2003 – Semipalatinsk

We flew up to Semipalatinsk near the Siberian border on a Yak-40. This is always an interesting experience. Operated by Kazakh Air, these are 40 seat workhorse jets, which were left behind by the Soviets when they departed from Kazakhstan in

1992. They have no hold, so all of our packing crates had to be carried on board. The plane was full, so one woman had to sit on the floor in the central aisle for the two hour flight. We were seated at the front of the plane on hard steel seats, with old loose cushions the only attempt at comfort. The passengers were fanning themselves frantically with magazines and newspapers as the searing heat inside the aircraft rose to dangerous levels. Our pilot, dressed in a dirty tee-shirt and jeans appeared to be arguing with the driver of a fuel tanker parked beside the plane. When he squeezed past us to enter the cockpit Elena asked him, in Russian, what was the problem. He explained that he'd tested the fuel in the tanker before filling up the plane and discovered it had been watered down! He'd ordered a new tanker to come and we'd have to wait until it arrived. As we digested this rather unnerving news a Kazakh pop singer, who was also a passenger in the plane, opened a huge bottle of vodka, took a deep slug, then proceeded to pass it around the entire aircraft. Elena, never a good flier at the best of times, was particularly grateful for this small swig of 'Kazakh courage'.

We were asked to get off first, on arrival at Semipalatinsk airport, where a contingent of local dignitaries had prepared a welcoming party on the tarmac. Young girls in Kazakh national dress presented bouquets of flowers to Kimberley and Elena. The Deputy Governor of the Semipalatinsk Region was there to greet us, along with the Deputy Governor of Semipalatinsk City. A large press contingent surged forward with cameras and microphones. Eighty-year-old Professor Balmukhanov (my 'father') and his wife Raufa were also there to meet us.

After registering at our hotel, we were taken with a police escort to the seat of Regional Government where a formal ceremony ensued. I outlined our objectives and explained that we want to raise public awareness in the West of the plight of the people of Semipalatinsk. *"Everyone has heard of the terrible tragedy of Chernobyl and the EU has poured millions in aid into that area. But that was a single nuclear explosion. No-one knows about Semipalatinsk and the nuclear holocaust which its people were subjected to"* I said.

To my complete surprise, the City's Deputy Governor announced that the regional parliament had voted to make me an Honorary Citizen of Semipalatinsk – only the 81st in its 300 year history and the first ever foreigner to receive such an honour. He explained that it was being awarded for my 'Tireless humanitarian efforts on behalf of the people of Semipalatinsk and the Polygon'. He pinned a medal on my chest, draped a sash around my shoulders and presented me with a framed certificate and special pass which, he assured me, grants me permanent freedom from taxation and arrest in Semipalatinsk. Receiving such an honour came as a bolt from the blue and I felt extremely proud to have been given such a high accolade from the people of Semipalatinsk. The Mayor then presented both Kimberley and myself with beautiful oil paintings of the city. A large press conference followed, then we left to visit the city's main hospital.

Kizat Kuzembayev stood proudly to attention as we entered his tiny ward in the cancer hospital in Semipalatinsk. Medals were pinned to his dressing gown indicating his status as an important war hero. He was 79 years old and suffering from terminal stomach cancer. In front of two other elderly cancer patients who share his room, he explained how he served with a reconnaissance unit in Danzig during W.W.II, receiving the Order of Glory, The Order of the Red Star and The Great Patriot's War medal in recognition of his bravery. These were the highest decorations for ordinary soldiers in the Soviet army.

But in 1953, he was one of 42 healthy young men selected by the Soviet military regime as human guinea pigs. The small group was taken to the village of Karaul in the remote steppe of East Kazakhstan. Local villagers had been evacuated and Mr Kuzembayev and his colleagues were ordered to leave the shelter of the village houses in which they were billeted, to watch an atomic explosion from a nearby hill. They were only 30 miles from the test site.

Mr Kuzembayev recalled the nuclear blast in vivid detail. He saw the sky turn red as if a huge fire had engulfed the landscape from horizon to horizon. As the ground trembled beneath his feet and the hellish roar of the atomic weapon swamped Karaul, he watched the fiery sky turn black, then grey, with piercing white and red spirals of flame shooting skywards, while the writhing stalk of the monstrous mushroom cloud unfolded. Later, KGB officers told his group that they would now have *no worries from the USA* as the Soviets had perfected their own atom bomb.

Mr Kuzembayev told us he felt fortunate to have lived to see his eightieth year. He was the only surviving member of this group of nuclear guinea pigs. The other 41 each died of cancer.

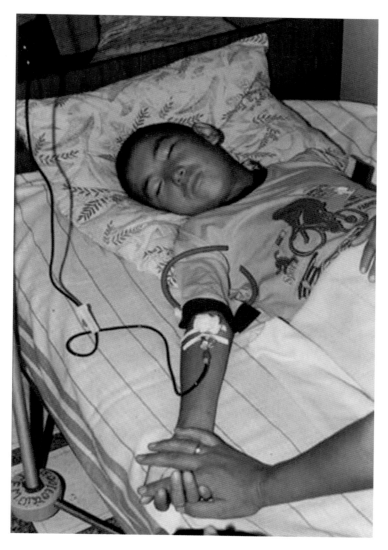

An outwardly fit teenager who collapsed whist playing football only to find he was suffering from chronic leukaemia

We told Mr Kuzembayev that we intended to visit Karaul on Thursday and he immediately asked the chief doctor – Marat Sandybaev – for permission to leave hospital for two days in order that he could meet us there. Despite his obvious illness, permission was granted.

Nike had provided us with the huge cartons of sweatshirts and baseball caps and they had also donated $5,000 in cash, which they asked me to distribute. I decided that $4,000 of this donation should be given to The Asian Credit Fund (ACF) to assist with their micro-credit loans programme in the Semipalatinsk area. This innovative programme turns the principle of traditional banking on its head. To qualify for a loan you have to be poor. The system involves helping deprived people at grassroots level by offering them credit to set up small or family businesses. We travelled to a side street in Semipalatinsk with Zhanna Zhakupova of the Asian Credit Fund to meet two of her clients who borrowed $1,000 and now run a successful sweet shop.

Later we visited the museum to victims of the nuclear tests. Housed in a small building near the Children's Hospital in Semipalatinsk, it is approached through a garden where, rather incongruously, all the old Soviet statues have been dumped. Visitors to the museum must pick their way gingerly past vast statues of Marx and Lenin and even giant, heroic-looking sculptures of Stalin, arms outstretched as if to embrace the citizens of Kazakhstan.

It is a great irony that a few yards away, rows and rows of glass jars contain the gruesome exhibits that bear grim witness to Stalin's legacy. Here in the horrific collection of the museum

Kizat Kuzembayev proudly displaying his war medals

are some of the victims of the nuclear tests. Deformed babies, born with their brains, intestines or spinal cords exposed. A boy born to a Soviet pilot and his wife who were working on the nuclear tests, with a single eye in the centre of his forehead – a perfect Cyclops – a harrowing reminder of the enormity of the radiation damage he and his parents were subjected to over a long period of time. This poor, malformed child was born alive and even survived for a few hours.

Thursday 7th August 2003 – Znamenka and Sarzhal

In the village of Znamenka, the local doctor introduced us to a group of patients. Znamenka was one of the villages worst affected by the nuclear tests and many of the inhabitants were ill. Cancers are rife. A group of elderly women recalled witnessing the first atomic explosions and seeing the mushroom clouds. They were told to stack bedding and furniture against their doors and windows to protect them from the shock waves, then to stand outside, away from any buildings, to watch the explosions.

A man of 25 was led towards us. His mother gripped his hand tightly. His head was almost entirely covered by a cancerous tumour, covering his eyes so that he could no longer see. Disconcertingly he said *"Ciao",* and then we learned that five years ago he was sent to Italy to have the tumour surgically removed, paid for by Japanese donors. Sadly, it began to grow again last year and his mother fears it will slowly kill him. She is only 57 years old, but looked like a woman of 80, the struggle to survive etched on her deeply tanned face.

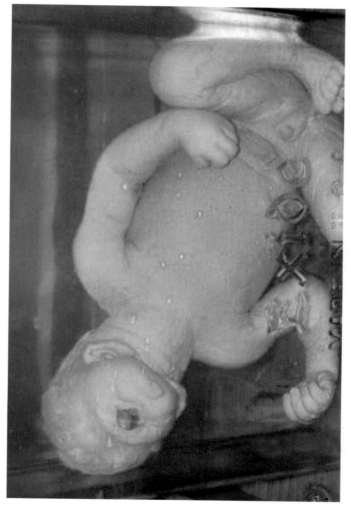

A severely deformed baby, affected by the radiation his parents were exposed to – he lived for a few hours

Witnesses to the mushroom clouds near Znamenka

Nearby, a mother held her young daughter who was born with a cleft palate and harelip. The child clutched a cuddly Loch Ness Monster given to her by Kimberley and tried to smile through her awful deformity. The doctor said that the cost of flying the child and her mother to the West for surgery is well beyond their means. We met other patients with mental retardation, cancers and deformities – the common currency of the Polygon.

After speeches from the village elders I gave the local head teacher $250 and a large crate of sweatshirts and caps from Nike, explaining that this was for the local children. As we clambered back into our Toyota Landcruiser, I reflected how even the generosity of Nike was insignificant in the face of such appalling suffering.

On across the endless Kazakh steppe our convoy trundled, leaving clouds of radioactive dust in our wake. Occasionally wild horses could be seen drinking from polluted lakes. Kazakh herdsmen on horseback tend their flocks of goats and sheep in the searing heat. Soon we reached the village of Sarzhal. This village was only ten miles from Ground Zero when the first nuclear tests were carried out. Later, the Soviet authorities moved it to 25 miles from the epicentre. Illness and disease have cut a swathe through the local population.

In the library, the village elders vented their fury at the Kazakh government's failure to provide adequate help. One tall gentleman, wearing a traditional Kazakh embroidered cap, roared his disgust, fingers jabbing the air. He shouted *"the government will not be happy until we are all dead and the problem has disappeared forever"*. He pointed through the window at the direction, from which the nuclear holocaust came and recalled the horror of the bomb blasts.

A local man rages at the Kazakh government's lack of action

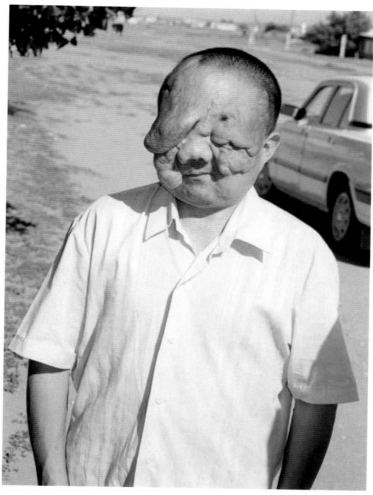

Beryk, a 26-year-old man with a cancerous growth covering his face, the result of exposure to radiation

A girl born with a cleft palate and harelip caused by genetic malformation in Znamenka

Another man of 80 came to the lectern. He was a decorated war veteran who served his country at the Battle of Stalingrad. In a dignified and quiet voice he explained that only two years ago he was a happily married grandfather with ten children and grandchildren. Now, 24 months later, his wife was dead from cancer, eight of his children and grand children had died from cancer and of his two remaining grandchildren, his eldest grand-daughter passed her business studies diploma in Semipalatinsk only last year, then committed suicide, overwhelmed by the tragedy engulfing her family. He said that he was forced to witness the first thermo-nuclear test.

A middle-aged woman began to sob quietly at the back of the hall. An elderly man wiped tears from his cheeks. I turned to look at Kimberley who was biting her lips, tears coursing down her face. *"How can we live on a pension of 8,000 tenge ($55) a month?"* he asked, referring to the special pension given to victims of the nuclear tests. On cue, the sky suddenly darkened and the library trembled as thunder roared across the steppe, almost as if the nuclear tests had begun again. A torrential downpour rattled on the corrugated roof, echoing the tears flowing inside.

In the village of Kainar, among the foothills of a low mountain range, villagers in national Kazakh costume had gathered outside a yurta, or nomadic tent, to welcome our group. Salty chunks of dried, curdled yoghurt were offered together with large wooden bowls filled with soured mare's milk. A sheep had been killed in our honour and I was asked to slice meat from the roasted head which sat forlornly on a wide dish, horns attached.

Traditionally the ears must be cut off first, as the greatest delicacy, and offered to the most honoured guest. Kimberley gracefully declined. Then slivers of meat from around the mouth and nostrils are cut and served in turn to each guest crouched at the low table. Endless toasts are offered, washed down with mare's milk or vodka. The wise choose vodka!

Soon the rest of the roasted sheep arrived, pieces of carved meat lying on alternate layers of thick yellow fat. Equally fatty horsemeat followed. The Kazakh villagers must survive temperatures of -40 degrees in winter and fat plays a large part in their daily diet. A lack of refrigeration to deal with the searing heat of summer means that milk and yoghurt must be soured and salted to survive. However, radiation has penetrated every layer of the food chain. The water supply is polluted, milk and meat are irradiated and vegetables absorb radiation from the soil. Not exactly a healthy diet!

It was pitch dark and we were exhausted. Our hosts assured us that the local village 'hotel' had been prepared for our visit. We were bemused to hear that a remote village on the steppe could boast an hotel, but our visions of a Las Vegas-style desert inn with luxury bedrooms and high-pressure showers were quickly dashed. Driving up a dark and dusty Kainar sidestreet, we shortly arrived at a walled enclosure behind which, we were told, a warm welcome awaited us. Tripping over abandoned car tyres and other assorted junk in the pitch black yard, we picked our way to the door of a long, tin-roofed hut. A young Kazakh man opened the door and beckoned us in. We were standing in the hallway of the village clinic, which had been emptied of patients prior to our arrival. This was the only place big enough to accommodate us and clearly the poor patients had been turfed out to make way for the foreign guests.

Our young guide pointed out the facilities. A metal basin hung precariously on one wall of the hallway. Above it, an old tin petrol can dangled from a piece of rope. Our guide tilted this ingenious device to demonstrate how water trickled from the petrol can into the basin beneath. This was for washing, he explained. Kimberley, Elena and Kamila were shown to a large dormitory, where filthy mattresses adorned a handful of rusty, iron beds. I was privileged to have my own single room, the only furniture being the iron bed, with a mattress that looked as if Genghis Khan himself had urinated on it as a child! A pungent odour hung in the air. Our guide told us that there was an outside toilet at the far end of the garden, but we decided not to risk falling into it in the dark. In any case, we had been invited to visit the village sauna in order that we could de-contaminate ourselves after our day in the Polygon, so we were hoping that better facilities might await us there. We dropped off our bags and boarded our Landcruiser for the short ride to the sauna. The village Akim led the way in his battered Lada.

Several dark deserted streets later we pulled up outside another rickety shed. This one had smoke and sparks belching from a tall brick chimney clearly signifying the existence of a sauna.

In Kazakhstan, like in Finland, saunas are a way of life. Despite the fact that summer temperatures often soar to +40 degrees centigrade, Kazakhs love nothing better than to sweat it out in a wood-fired sauna. Of course, there was no electricity in the sauna, or indeed anywhere else in Kainar. Kamila, Kimberley, Elena and I stumbled into the dark shed and lit several candles. The smell of wood smoke filled the air and searing heat pulsed from the sauna room. Despite the almost pitch darkness, the three women decided to undress in the actual sauna room itself, while I used the tiny foyer. Suitably wrapped in an old towel provided by the village Akim, I was about to knock on the sauna door to establish whether it was safe to enter, when the outside door burst open to reveal a young, wild-looking Kazakh man. He was gesticulating and jabbering madly in Kazakh and was clearly drunk as a skunk. Before I could stop him, he had pushed his way past me and threw open the door to the sauna room. He was met with squeals of dismay by the three women, followed by a torrent of angry Kazakh from Kamila.

The drunk man, it transpired, was in charge of our sauna. He had been asked to set the fire and get the sauna working late at night for us to use and, as a reward, had been given a litre of vodka. He had obviously consumed the entire bottle before deciding to pay his respects to the almost naked foreign visitors. As we sat sweating out radiation in the darkness, we could hear our drunk friend singing loudly behind the sauna, as he piled more and more logs into the roaring furnace at our backs.

Our sauna adventures were not quite over either. We found a huge barrel of water poised precariously on the flat roof of the sauna, from which protruded a short hose. By pulling out a plug from the end of this hose it was possible to get a fairly rapid trickle of cold water in the form of a sort of shower. One by one we discreetly showered in the pitch darkness under this DIY device. We dried ourselves and got dressed before stumbling outside to search for the village Akim who had promised to come for us in his Lada. There was no sign of life. Even the drunk sauna attendant had disappeared. In the distance a dog barked. A million stars sparkled in the great steppe sky. But where were we? We knew our so-called 'hotel' was only a few streets away, but the streets are un-paved, un-named and unlit. We hadn't a clue which way to go. An hour passed. We were beginning to feel the cold of the night creeping into our freshly sauna-ed bones when at last, we could hear the sound of a car approaching. It was the Akim. He apologised profusely for being late. Never have four people clambered into a Lada with such enthusiasm and soon we were back in our 'hotel' where a fitful sleep awaited us.

Friday 8th August 2003 – Kainar

The cemetery just outside Kainar is almost bigger than the village itself. Grave after grave bears the pictures of young men and women, victims of cancer or suicide. The inscriptions are poignant. One young woman died at the age of 20. Her name was Orazken Malkarbay. On her tomb is written 'She did not reach her 21st Spring and left us suddenly. 'Crying forever'. Her Father.' 'Suddenly' is a Kazakh euphemism for suicide, our guide explains.

The village hall in Kainar was filled to overflowing. More than 500 people had turned out to greet us and tell us of their suffering. Again we handed over gifts from Nike and the local

The cemetery outside Kainar overflows with the graves of young suicide victims

Akim responded by presenting Kimberley with a horse. Kimberley was completely overwhelmed by the generosity of her gift and although very grateful for it, her thoughts did turn to how she was going to look after a horse during her stay in Kazakhstan, or, worse still, get it through customs at Heathrow!

Some heated exchanges began between the villagers and the local politicians. By now we were three hours behind schedule. Sixteen scientists from the National Nuclear Research Centre in Kurchatov were waiting for us at the Atomic Lake. They had brought protective clothing and gallons of water to wash us down after our visit. However, our guide had a better idea. He had agreed to a suggestion from a villager that we should take a shortcut across the steppe, cutting our journey time to the Atomic Lake in half. We set off in a convoy of vehicles across the grass-covered plains, dust billowing behind us.

The journey by road should have taken just under two hours. After four hours bumping across the prairie we realised we were lost. Soon we spotted a small ridge rising from the plain and made our way towards it, hoping to get a better view of our surroundings from the summit. The ridge had a broken fence surrounding it, which should have sounded some alarms for us, but it was only when I got out of our Landcruiser and walked to the top of the ridge that the full horror of our situation dawned on me. I was staring into an atomic bomb crater!

We had inadvertently stumbled across one of the nuclear bomb test sites, which are lethally dangerous and strictly prohibited to all access. Dr Sandybaev came running up waving his Geiger counter. *"It's registering 160 roentgens – a*

An elderly villager joins Kimberley and the horse she was presented with in Kainar

lethal dose" he shouted, *"we have to get out of here quickly."*[1]
We set off again at high speed, bouncing across the uneven terrain.

After an hour we stopped for a comfort break when suddenly I noticed smoke billowing from underneath the Landcruiser. Prairie grass had wound itself tightly around the drive shaft and ignited against the hot exhaust. Our driver dived under the vehicle with a cloth. I threw bottles of water to him. The flames were licking dangerously close to the fuel pipe and already the tall grass beneath the car had caught fire. Kamila, Kimberley, Elena and I beat out the grass fire using rubber car mats pulled from the Landcruiser. For five minutes the driver fought the blaze under the vehicle, finally emerging blackened with smoke, his right hand severely scorched. He had almost certainly saved our lives.

Around 9.00pm we found a Kazakh herdsman on horseback and asked him for directions. He told us to follow a distant line of broken poles, which once brought power across the steppe to the nuclear test sites. After another hour we found the crumbling township which once housed the Soviet military guards and KGB personnel. Our Geiger counter was still recording abnormally high levels of radioactivity. It was past midnight before we finally discovered an asphalt road and headed for a small village where we were able to awaken the owner of the only petrol tank for miles around. We refilled the Landcruiser and headed back towards some kind of

---

1. Roentgens were named after Wilhelm Konrad Roentgen who discovered x-ray in 1895. Roentgen is the unit used to measure exposure to x-rays or gamma rays and although there are no safe levels, it is widely believed that anything above 35 is highly dangerous dose.

One of the atomic craters still posing a dangerous threat in the Polygon

civilisation. Unbelievably, as we neared the city of Semipalatinsk in the wee small hours of the morning, we suddenly came across two cars waiting for us at the roadside, with a small feast of caviar and vodka laid out, picnic-style, to celebrate our survival. Word had somehow been sent ahead and the Kazakhs, much relieved that we had not disappeared forever in the endless steppe, were determined to drink to our adventure, no matter what time it was!

Saturday 9th August 2003 – Karaul

Our final village visit in the Polygon was to Karaul. In the medical centre we were ushered into the room of a beautiful fourteen year old girl called Aigerim. She stood as we entered. She was wearing a trendy tee shirt with 'love 7' emblazoned on the front and a pair of flared jeans. She had incredibly sad eyes. The chief doctor explained that, like all other children in the area, Aigerim has chronic anaemia. However, they had been unable to get her blood back to normal and she now had chronic hepatitis, kidney failure and the onset of scoliosis - the condition where the spine can no longer bear the weight of the head and begins to bend painfully. Aigerim listened to our expressions of sympathy, her sad eyes telling us that she only yearns to be like any other teenage girl, away from this place of pain and suffering.

Aigerim's proud silence played on my mind for the rest of the visit to Kazakhstan. Her desperation masked by steely determination was so real I could almost feel it and it served only to strengthen my resolve to do even more to try to alleviate the ongoing suffering and despair these people are forced to endure. Later I sent Kamila the funds to buy Aigerim a CD player and some rock CDs from the West to cheer her up.

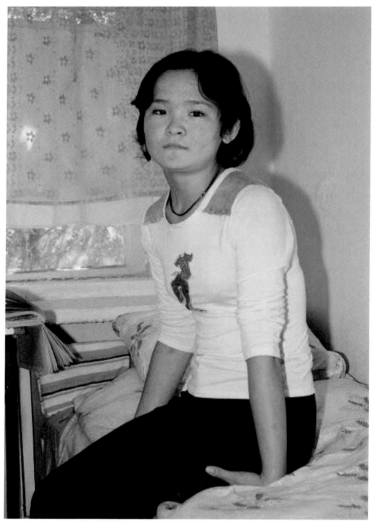

Aigerim, a 14-year-old girl suffering from chronic anaemia, chronic hepatitis, kidney disease and scoliosis, Karaul

Sunday 10th August 2003 – Almaty

Having distributed all of our aid, our return to Almaty on the dreaded Yak-40 was considerably easier than our journey here. We had averaged around three hours sleep each night during our trip. We were all exhausted, but elated that we had achieved our key objectives. We had taken around 1,000 photos and aimed to mount a major touring exhibition which we had agreed we would take to the Scottish Parliament in Edinburgh, to Westminster, to the European Parliament, to the UN Headquarters in New York and finally to Kazakhstan itself. By doing so, we hoped to raise awareness amongst key legislators and also to raise sponsorship from sales of a book of photos, profits from which would go to the people of Semipalatinsk.

2004 – Telling the Story

The Exhibitions

From experience gained organising the previous photo exhibitions in Scotland, Brussels and Ireland, I realised that a new series of exhibitions required serious sponsorship. I set about writing to dozens of leading Scottish business Executives, telling them about Semipalatinsk and setting out the case for financial assistance for my project. The response was overwhelming. Unilever, Nike, Lloyds TSB Scotland, Scottish & Newcastle and several individuals, all gave generous donations.

It was clear that I needed a vehicle for these donations and a Scottish charity immediately sprang to mind. For a long time I had admired the work of Mercy Corps Scotland. I knew that they had an office in America and that their HQ was in Edinburgh and that they supported some charitable activity in Semipalatinsk. It seemed like a marriage made in heaven!

I contacted their Scottish Director, Jane Salmonson, and asked if she was prepared to set up a special Semipalatinsk Fund into which I could pour donations. Jane readily agreed and in return, I pledged financial help for Mercy Corp's Asia Credit Fund operation in Semipalatinsk. It is their brilliant micro-loans initiative, to whom I'd previously given $4,000 from Nike, which lends money to poor people to help them help themselves out of poverty.

The Kazakh Government, through their UK and EU Ambassadors, agreed to meet the costs of printing and sending out invitations to the exhibitions and the cost of wine and canapés for the opening receptions. They also arranged for Air Astana to fly the exhibition material free of charge to Kazakhstan when we took the show to Almaty, Astana and Semipalatinsk.

With the financial backing secured, working with my PR assistant Elaine McKean from Indigo in Edinburgh, we selected around 30 of the best photos from the 1,000 taken on our last visit to the Polygon and employed One World Design to transpose the photo exhibition onto three enormous folding screens. We also created a campaign leaflet and powerpoint presentation to support the exhibition, as a call for action to contribute to the aid fund.

With intense work involving my ever-faithful parliamentary staff Luisa Strani, Lisa Rose and Belinda Don, we now set about arranging a series of exhibitions and presentations under the title 'CRYING FOREVER'.

The first event was held in the Scottish Parliament in Edinburgh, attended by many parliamentarians and representatives of NGOs (Non-Government Organisations), as well as journalists. Next, the Department for International Development (DfID) mounted our exhibition in its headquarters in Whitehall. Again there was a great attendance including many senior staff from a wide range of foreign embassies. Our EU tour ended in the European Parliament in Brussels, where Konstantin Zhigalov – Kazakh Ambassador to the EU - joined me in giving an opening address.

At each event we distributed specially published 'Crying Forever' leaflets, giving details of how to make financial donations to Mercy Corp Scotland's Semipalatinsk Fund.

A panel from the 'Crying Forever' exhibition

Following the event in Brussels, the European Commission official dealing with Central Asia approached me to say that he was leaving his job to take up a new post in Africa. However, he had been so moved by my presentation that he intended to donate €1,000 from his own private funds, to help the people of Semipalatinsk.

We now began to organise the more complicated series of exhibitions we were planning for Kazakhstan. I felt that it was necessary to show the photos and tell the story of Semipalatinsk to the Kazakhs themselves, many of whom are unaware of the full details of what happened on their territory at the hands of the Soviets. I recalled taking around 30 reels of film to be developed in a photo shop in Almaty following our visit to the Polygon in 2003. When we returned to collect the photos the next day, the shop staff were keen to find out where the pictures had been taken. They were deeply shocked by some of the images and couldn't believe such a catastrophe had occurred within their own country. I was also keen to take the exhibition to the villages in the Polygon where most of the photos had been taken, to show the villagers what we were doing in their name. We received fantastic help and encouragement from Ambassador Zhigalov who undertook to make all the necessary arrangements for our next visit to Kazakhstan.

One Thursday evening in March 2004, as I was flying back to Scotland from Strasbourg, I picked up a copy of the Herald Tribune and read an intriguing ad which aroused my curiosity. Under the heading 'The Power of Purpose', the advertisement invited entries for a worldwide essay competition 'designed to investigate the evidence and benefits of purpose in the world around us'. Submitted essays had to be 3,000 words long and would be judged by an international panel of academics and university professors. The competition was sponsored by the US-based John Templeton Foundation who were offering a total of $500,000 in prize money.

I tore out the ad and over the next two weekends, wrote 3,000 words about Semipalatinsk entitled 'Crying Forever' and emailed it to the US as my official entry to The Power of Purpose Essay Competition. I received an email by return informing me that my entry had been accepted and that I would hear nothing further unless I was notified that I had won a prize.

It was many weeks later, in early September, that I received a conference call from New York at eight o'clock on a Friday evening. I had just returned to my home in Scotland and was leafing through the usual mountain of mail which had accumulated during my absence. Pat, my wife, also just back from her work as a radio editor at the BBC, was preparing dinner. I picked up the phone at the second ring to hear an American woman's voice informing me that *"This is a conference call from The Power of Purpose International Essay Competition"*.

It transpired that two of the international panel of judges were on the line to inform me that I had won overall second prize in the competition and that a cheque for $50,000 would be handed over to me at a special ceremony in New York in two weeks' time. As I sat dumbstruck at this news, Pat appeared in the doorway and said *"Your dinner is ready. Who are you phoning?"* I signalled to her that it was an important call and covering the mouthpiece with my hand, whispered *"It's a call* *from the States. I've won $50,000".* Knowing nothing of the competition or of the fact that I had entered an essay, Pat said *"It's a scam. Hang up!"*

However, I knew it wasn't a scam and I could hear the great excitement in the voices of the two judges on the other side of the Atlantic as they explained how moved they had been by my essay and how this was exactly what 'The Power of Purpose' was all about.

When I pointed out that I would not be able to attend the award ceremony in New York as I was actually heading back to Kazakhstan to lead a small team of election observers to the forthcoming elections to the Kazakh Majilis (Parliament), they expressed their disappointment but said they would forward the $50,000 cheque to me in Scotland. They said that my essay would be extensively published in US broadsheets and in TIME magazine and ultimately in a book of the winning essays. I was stunned by this news. I thanked them warmly and rushed through to the kitchen to tell Pat. With a feeling of great excitement and elation we sat down and worked out how we could put this unexpected windfall to best use for the people of Semipalatinsk.

We both quickly agreed that the entire $50,000 should be donated to Mercy Corps Scotland with specific instructions on how it should be distributed to the victims of the Soviet nuclear tests. Our excitement was fantastic. I couldn't wait to inform Mercy Corps, although I'd been sworn to secrecy until the day of the award ceremony by the Templeton Foundation.

I decided that the $50,000 should be split two ways. $25,000 should go to the Asia Credit Fund, for helping people living in

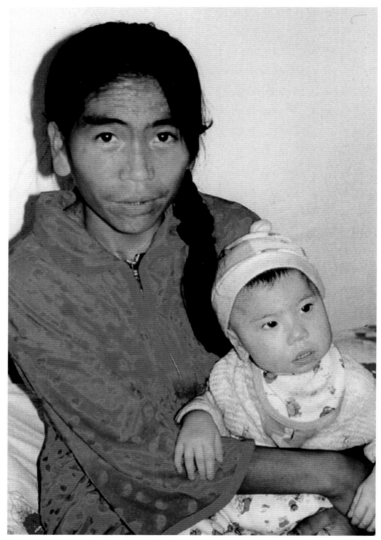

Many women in the Polygon are afraid to become pregnant in case they give birth to mentally-deficient babies, such as this little girl with its mother

the Polygon to help themselves out of poverty, while the other $25,000 should go to the Oncology Hospital in Semipalatinsk to help them purchase a mobile scanner for diagnosing cancer in the remote Kazakh villages.

Two weeks later, as 'The Power of Purpose' award ceremony took place in New York and two senior executives of Mercy Corps accepted the $50,000 cheque on my behalf, I was already in Kazakhstan, heading up a team of election observers. Part of our mission included a meeting with President Nazarbayev and it seemed to me an ideal opportunity to raise the question of Semipalatinsk. The meeting took place in the Presidential Palace in Astana and lasted for over an hour.

The President outlined the dynamic nature of the Kazakh economy. *"Kazakhstan wants to live in the modern world and be an active partner in the modern world"* he said. He spoke of how the country, only thirteen years since the end of the Soviet system, had secured stability and independence, a well developed economy and democracy. He said that he was pursuing a policy of 'liberalisation from the top', and recalled that only six years ago many parts of Kazakhstan had endured primitive conditions with people setting fires in the streets in order to cook their meals. Rapid economic change has seen massive improvements to infrastructure throughout the country and the many diverse ethnic and religious communities live together peacefully and in a free and tolerant society. *"Even Russia says we're moving too fast!"* he said.

President Nazarbayev said that he had to introduce democracy from scratch after the fall of the Soviet administration. He personally had promoted the formation of a multiparty system and the establishment of various political parties in Kazakhstan, knowing full well that some of them would become critics of his policies. This was the nature of democracy. However, he said that Kazakhstan has witnessed the best and the worst of the election process during this campaign. Although enormous work had been undertaken to train officials and to prepare for the introduction of e-voting, nevertheless *"everyone is still scared of electronic voting"*.

When I challenged him about the new ASAR Party led by his daughter Dariga, President Nazarbayev said that he would await the verdict of the electorate on ASAR and, in any case, would not answer questions on behalf of his daughter. *"She is a grown up and can answer for herself"* he said. Next, I asked the President about Semipalatinsk. I told him that I had just won $50,000 and was intent on giving this to the Asia Credit Fund and the Oncology Hospital in Semipalatinsk. Indeed, I asked the President if he was prepared to match the $25,000 I was giving to the Oncology Hospital.

President Nazarbayev said he was well aware of the extensive work I had done for the people of Semipalatinsk and he thanked me warmly on behalf of all the citizens of Kazakhstan for my efforts. He congratulated me on the $50,000 prize and welcomed the news that I would donate all of it to the victims of the Soviet nuclear tests. He said that he had personally set up a 'Nazarbayev Fund' earmarked for providing aid to the people of Semipalatinsk and the Polygon and he would examine whether he could match-fund my $25,000 donation to the Oncology Hospital from this source.

2005 – A Mission of Hope

All the arrangements for the photo exhibitions in Kazakhstan were now in place. I had informed the Asia Credit Fund and Dr Sandybaev at the Oncology Centre in Semipalatinsk that bank transfers for $25,000 each were in the process of being completed. The exhibition 'wheelie-bins' were winging their way to Almaty courtesy of Air Astana and Elena and Kimberley had re-arranged their diaries to make time for Kazakhstan. Our next mission was underway.

Monday 18th July 2005 – Almaty

The flight from Moscow was two hours late and finally departed for Almaty at 1:30 am. Air Astana economy class is not to be recommended for those seeking a restful slumber. The squalling baby, who sits behind me on every flight, was there again! It must collect loads of air miles! I put on a mask and slumped against my tiny pillow to try to get some sleep on the five-hour flight. But at 2:00 am the crew served drinks, with dinner following at 2:30 am. At 3:00 am they served coffee and at 3:30 am they came around with headphones! I put mine on just to drown out the noise.

I awoke from a deep sleep lasting only one hour to see the dawn breaking in spectacular fashion over the polluted Aral Sea. We were coming in to land in Almaty. I was met at the gate and escorted to the VIP lounge. My Kazakh 'sister' – Kamila, Sulushash (her daughter) and Elena were all there to meet me, as were two civil servants from the Majilis (Parliament) and a lady from the Akimat (Mayoral office) of Almaty. A big reception committee indeed!

Struan and Professor Balmukhanov outside his Dacha, Almaty

We headed off to the Dostyk Hotel. There was heavy rain yesterday, Kamila explained, so everything has been washed clean in the city for my arrival. Perfect blue skies, snow-capped mountains, blue onion domes on the Mosques. What a beautiful city!

I had two hours' sleep in the Dostyk hotel then headed off to a Travel Agency to collect tickets for our internal flights. We had lunch in the Theater Restaurant with John Penny (Second in Command to Ambassador Allan Waddams in the European Commission Office), plus UK Ambassador James Sharpe and Anna Bramwell – newly arrived European Commission Head of the Kazakh Desk. The European Commission had generously put €1,500 sponsorship towards my photo exhibition and I took the opportunity to thank them and discuss the current political situation in Central Asia with these experts.

After lunch we drove to the Dacha (holiday bungalow) of my Kazakh 'father', Professor Balmukhanov on the outskirts of Almaty, nestling in a grove of apple trees on the mountain-side. A traditional wood-burning samovar was bubbling in the garden, filled with delicious green tea. His wife, Raufa had prepared a huge feast of cakes and fruit and had a table groaning under the weight of it all. Toasts were made with Kazakh brandy.

In the evening we were guests at Ambassador Sharpe's party to say goodbye to DfID (The Department for International Development – Whitehall), after thirteen years of work in Kazakhstan, involving primary health care reform, the development of civil society and planning for sustainable land use in the Semipalatinsk area. They now regard their task completed. I wished I could be so confident!

Tuesday 19th July 2005 – Almaty

I visited the Asian Credit Fund in Tole bi Street, Almaty. Zhana Zhakupova, the director, was there to greet us together with all 25 of her HQ staff, most of whom are women. The ACF's policy of lending money to the poor, is helping families to survive and create wage income through the setting up of small businesses, particularly in areas like Semipalatinsk, where there is little or no inward investment and therefore few job opportunities.

Last time I was in Semipalatinsk in 2003 I brought ACF $4,000 from Nike. This time I had given them $25,000 – half of my $50,000 'Power of Purpose' essay competition prize, which I channelled to them via Mercy Corps. Zhana informed me that the money had initially gone towards a sausage factory in Semipalatinsk. Apparently before the Soviets departed in 1991, Semipalatinsk boasted one of the most famous sausage factories in the USSR. However, the Soviets stripped out all the equipment and took it back to Russia with them, leaving hundreds of skilled Kazakh sausage-makers unemployed.

Recently, a local entrepreneur has started up the factory again, employing a few people in his back kitchen. He asked the ACF for a loan and has now expanded to employ 25 people. My $25,000 will provide him with the capacity to expand further employing another twelve people. He will then repay the loan to ACF, enabling the cash to be recycled and used to create other small businesses in Semipalatinsk.

ACF provide business advice on products, marketing and sales as well as even providing advice on hygiene and welfare. They have an amazing rate of repayment, which puts the big

A sweet shop in Semipalatinsk helped by the Asian Credit Fund

High Street banks to shame. Only 0.002% of loans are written off. In fact, repayment default in the Semipalatinsk area is 0.000%. The average age of people receiving an ACF loan is 43, of whom 53% are women. Twenty-one per cent of their loans are in production-based enterprises, 19% in services and 60% in trade, such as shops and small stores.

After lunch we were driven to the Akimat for a press conference. As always there was a huge turnout of the national and regional mass media. We were joined by Erzhan Rakhmetov, the Member of the Majilis for Semipalatinsk. Erzhan is an old friend who has accompanied me on several visits to the Polygon. He and I did all the talking, with Elena translating.

One woman from one of the two independent TV stations was interested only in my views on the forthcoming presidential elections and the government crackdown on NGOs and the media. I said that I was prepared to answer her, despite this being a distraction from my visit and from the topic of the Polygon. I told her that the view in Europe was that Kazakhstan was a well run and stable country and an excellent partner for the West in a zone of instability. I said that even independent opinion polls had demonstrated that the President is popular and will easily win the presidential elections in December.

In my opinion there was no need for tough measures against the media and opposition parties. Such measures were counterproductive. However, there was no doubt that some subversive groups had used the cover of NGOs for activities aimed at de-stabilising Kazakhstan. This could not be tolerated in any democracy and I understood the need for a crackdown on such organisations. I said that the government must nevertheless be careful not to tar all NGOs with the same brush. The big, international NGOs should not face tougher restrictions.

Most of the questions were about my mission to Semipalatinsk and my $50,000 donation. I explained that I had also successfully amended the EU budget three years ago to reallocate €4 million to the Tacis fund for aiding the victims of the Soviet nuclear tests in Semipalatinsk. I said that I was dismayed to discover last time I was here, that most of this money had been paid to Western consultants. As a result, I had written to the then Commissioner Chris Patten asking if a re-submission from the Kazakh Government could enable up to half of this Tacis money to be redirected to the oncology hospital in Semipalatinsk.

Tacis criteria stipulates that the money must only be used for poverty alleviation. However, I explained that where the breadwinner in a family has died of cancer and the remaining spouse develops breast cancer, then restoring that person quickly to good health so that they can earn money and care for their children is poverty alleviation. Chris Patten had agreed with this view and Anna Bramwell from the Kazakh Desk in the Commission Office in Almaty had told me yesterday that this idea is currently being considered by the Commission.

Next our team went to the Arman Cinema in Almaty where the photo exhibition was taking place. It is a functioning multiplex and had several feature films showing. Many young people were coming and going in the foyer, where our two civil servants from the Majilis watched intently as I demonstrated how to set up the three exhibition panels. For the rest of the week they became experts in doing this themselves, erecting and dismantling the panels in minutes. We soon had all three screens set up in the main foyer and we went to the first floor lounge area to test the powerpoint presentation and the sound system. All was OK.

At 7:00 pm we returned to the cinema to greet the hundreds of invited guests. People were provided with a drink on arrival and ushered up to the first floor lounge after looking at the exhibition panels. I was introduced by a lady from the Akimat to a packed audience with many film crews, radio journalists and reporters and began my powerpoint presentation with Elena translating. The Japanese Ambassador was present, as were two senior staff from the US embassy. A famous Kazakh singer, apparently a favourite of Stalin and allegedly his mistress, now aged 82, whom I met in 2003 in Semipalatinsk, was also there. She was dressed in a crisp white military tunic bedecked with her Soviet medals. She said to me that it was wrong to criticise the Soviet regime for many things, but that she fully understood that using the people of the Polygon as human guinea pigs had been a great crime.

Afterwards the guests were provided with food and drink and my team were ushered to a VIP lounge for a private dinner where again many toasts were given in Kazakh vodka and brandy.

Wednesday 20th July 2005 – Astana

I went down to breakfast in the Dostyk Hotel at 9:30 am and was helping myself to fresh fruit and yoghurt when Kimberley

A typical operating theatre in the oncology unit, in much need of modernisation, Semipalatinsk

grabbed me from behind. She had flown in to Almaty during the night from L.A. and had been met by Elena and Kamila. She was in good form and excited to be back in Kazakhstan.

At 10.45am we left for the airport to catch our flight to Astana. This was a regular Air Astana flight in a decent-sized and fairly new passenger jetliner. We arrived in Astana to be met by a trio of tall, beautiful Kazakh girls dressed in national costume. Each of us was presented with a huge bouquet of flowers before being whisked off to the Comfort Hotel at ultra-high speed in a convoy of cars supplied by the Majilis. It was blisteringly hot – around 40 degrees. Elena and I had only ten minutes to dump our stuff in our hotel rooms, change into suits and posh clothes and then head to the Majilis for a meeting with the Deputy Speaker.

Astana is a city springing from the desert. Lavish new buildings in futuristic shapes and sizes are rising amidst a sea of cranes and scaffolding. The new capital boasts parks and fountains, lakes and rivers. Clearly a lot of investment is going into the creation of President Nazarbayev's pet project. We were driven to the Majilis, or new parliament. This massive edifice, complete with thousands of tonnes of coloured marble and sparkling chandeliers, nestles in the middle of a complex of brand new buildings including the Senate and the Supreme Court. The whole compound is dominated by a grandiose building – the new presidential palace.

Inside the Majilis we were taken to the 20th floor and into a room where a large squad of journalists had assembled to cover my meeting with the Deputy Speaker. He arrived shortly – a tall, thin and distinguished gentleman of Russian rather than Kazakh appearance as his name, Sergey Dyachenko, bore testament. He is also Co-chairman of the Kazakhstan-EU inter-parliamentary co-operation committee. He thanked me warmly for all of my work in Semipalatinsk and for the $50,000 donation. He said I was renowned throughout Kazakhstan for my humanitarian work.

We soon turned to wider EU-Kazakh affairs. I said that I felt the President was popular with the people and that each time I visit Kazakhstan it is obvious to see the major improvements that are being made. I said, however, that it would be more acceptable to us in the EU if President Nazarbayev was to win a fair and open election with a realistic majority of say 65%, rather than a completely unreal majority of say 90%.

The Deputy Speaker said he understood my point entirely and agreed with me. I also said that I was alarmed at crackdowns on the media and opposition parties and said that we believed in the EU that elections had not only to be free and fair, but must also be seen to be free and fair. Mr Dyachenko defended the recent legislation approved by the Majilis but again agreed with me that Western perceptions of the election were important in ensuring that there was no destabilisation of the country following the result.

I then tackled him on the Presidential decree that demanded all international flights should be routed to Astana rather than Almaty. I said that this was ludicrous and that as a Conservative, I could never agree with attempts to interfere with the market. I said that it was clear that Astana was expanding exponentially and would, in due course, attract international flights in any case. However, if carriers wished to fly to Almaty they must be permitted to do so.

ОСТРОВ СЕМИПАЛАТИНСК

С некоторых пор о проблемах Семипалатинского полигона в Казахстане хорошо осведомлены в Европарламенте. Между тем, по мнению почетного гражданина Семипалатинска Струана Стивенсона, сами казахстанцы до сих пор имеют лишь поверхностное представление об истинных масштабах многочисленных бед жителей бывшего полигона. А это не только низкий уровень экономики, стабильно высокий уровень онкологических заболеваний, но и до сих пор не изученная проблема генных изменений организма, от которых страдает уже не одно поколение региона

БОГАТО СЕЙДАХМЕТОВА

Струан Стивенсон уже в четвертый раз посещает этот регион. Он депутат Европейского парламента от Шотландии (коллеги в шутку называют его депутатом от Семипалатинска), заместитель председателя фракции Европейского парламента «Европейская народная партия (христиан-демократы)» и европейских демократов.

В первый раз о проблеме полигона Струан Стивенсон узнал в 1991 году, став депутатом Европарламента, от Камилы Магтымовой — представителя казахстанской части программы TACIS.

■ Выставка

Семипалатинская трагедия глазами иностранца

Вчера в Алматы открылась выставка депутата Европарламента Струана Стивенсона. В течение нескольких лет шотландец посещал Семипалатинский регион и на любительских фото запечатлел страшные последствия ядерных испытаний.

Оксана СВЕЖЕНЦЕВА

Struan's visit to Kazakhstan was widely reported

94

To my surprise, once again Mr Dyachenko said he agreed with me. In fact, he said he was astonished at how much we saw eye to eye on all matters we had discussed. At this point I presented him with a bottle of Parliamentary Whisky as a gift. Of course my gesture immediately attracted the attention of the film crews and, inevitably, this was the one bit of footage shown all across Kazakhstan on the evening news! Mr Dyachenko presented me with a Kazakh figurine in a wooden presentation case.

By now it was 5.15pm and we raced off to have a late lunch with representatives of the Akimat in Astana. The lady Akim and her senior officials had a lavish spread waiting for us, with young sturgeon, salmon caviar and many other wonderful local delicacies. As I was due to make my presentation shortly afterwards, I eschewed the many offers of wine, vodka and brandy.

At 7.00pm we arrived at the major public hall where the exhibition had been set up. It was still desperately hot. I was bathed in sweat! The panels had been erected in the foyer and the powerpoint presentation was to be delivered in a vast, tiered and un-air-conditioned auditorium. Only around 70 people had turned up.

Kamila Magzieva immediately launched an attack on the representatives of the Ministry of Foreign Affairs, whom she accused of being lazy and indolent and not sending out the invitations. They rounded on her and a noisy argument ensued. I told them all to calm down and took to the stage with Elena to deliver my one-hour presentation. At the end I invited Kimberley to take the floor.

Kimberley immediately electrified the audience by saying that if even 25% of the money being spent in developing Astana could be diverted to the Polygon, they could resolve many of the problems affecting the nuclear test victims! There was a stunned silence amongst the audience of civil servants, politicians and apparatchiks. That night, Kimberley's speech was on every TV channel!

Back at the Comfort Hotel at 10:00 pm, I received a telephone call on my mobile from Konstantin Zhigalov, Kazakh Ambassador to the EU. Clearly he'd heard that there had been a shouting match between Kamila and the Ministry officials and he was concerned in case things had gone pear-shaped. I assured him that all was OK and that an audience of 70 in Astana in mid-July was not too bad, given that it is the administrative capital of Kazakhstan and most people have gone on holiday, now that the parliament in recess.

Thursday 21st July 2005 – Semipalatinsk

We checked out of the hotel early and headed for the airport to catch our 9:30 am flight to Semipalatinsk. In the splendid facilities of the VIP lounge in the spanking new airport, we were lulled into a false sense of security, which was quickly shattered when we encountered our plane! A VIP minibus whisked us along the runway towards a huge, shining Air Astana jet. Sadly, it whizzed past this comfortable airliner and made for a tiny, rusty Antonov 24. These were built 40 years ago in the USSR. They are twin prop aircraft, which have certainly seen better days.

We boarded up a steel ladder at the rear of the plane. Inside, an old 'stair runner' carpet covered the central aisle. Bits of old carpet were also draped on every seat. Patches of Scotch Tape covered a multitude of scars and holes in the cabin ceiling. Elena, never a good flier at the best of times, freaked out! She went forward to the cockpit and asked the pilot what age the plane was. He said that although it was 30 years old it was totally safe and that he flown it thousands of times. Erzhan Rakhmetov, the local MP, reassured Elena that these twin prop aircraft are OK, because they can fly on one engine and even glide to a safe landing with no engines! (A cursory search of the internet later revealed that the Antonov 24 fleet of aircraft has suffered no fewer than 160 total loss crashes, with 1,671 fatalities! So much for a 'perfectly safe' aircraft.)

Although the flight to Semipalatinsk on this rusty war-horse was smooth enough, the takeoff and landing were both turbulent due to the heat and thermals in the middle of the Kazakh steppe. The landing, in particular, had passengers retching into sick bags and Elena gripping my hand with her sweaty palms!

However, we survived! As always at Semipalatinsk, we could see a huge welcoming party waiting for us on the runway. There was my old friend, the Akim Nurlan Omorov as well as Dr Sandybaev, Director of the Oncology Centre. Once again we were presented with huge bouquets of flowers by beautiful local girls in national costume. Straight away we had to do interviews with TV and radio reporters who were waiting for us at the airport.

We set off for the Hotel Binar, the place we always stay. To my surprise, they had built a new wing, which included a presidential suite. This had been allocated to me, complete with sauna and massive sitting room. However, hot water only appeared in the evenings and the new shower leaked all over the bathroom floor! A sumptuous lunch of sturgeon and the inevitable horsemeat awaited us in the sweltering dining room. Lavish toasts were drunk to celebrate my return to Semipalatinsk.

Following lunch we set off in a convoy, with a police escort, to visit projects funded by the Asian Credit Fund. An elderly couple who told us they had five children and ten grandchildren had been given a loan to open a small grocery shop. They had made a success of this and were now able to sustain their family. Kimberley and I purchased 2,000 tenge (around €10) worth of sweets to hand out to children in the villages, which we will visit tomorrow. This really pleased them, as it seemed like a major purchase.

Then we drove to the former Soviet Youth Building which now houses a series of projects to create jobs and small businesses. We were taken inside by a bearded guy, with long black hair and gold earrings. He wanted us to see his newly refurbished recording studios. He is a rock musician and music teacher and has borrowed money from the ACF to create what he claims is the best recording studio in Kazakhstan, designed and fitted out by scientists from the nuclear centre at Kurchatov. Thank God the nuclear scientists are now turning their hand to something more productive!

Next we went to the Oncology Centre. This has been the focus of my campaign for some years and I was delighted and astonished to be met by Dr Marat Sandybaev and his entire hospital staff of over 200, mostly women. They had gathered in the central waiting room of the hospital to greet us and again large bouquets of flowers were handed over. In fact we had brought the bouquets previously given to us at the airport, to the hospital, to hand out to the patients, so there was a sort of exchange of bouquets at this point!

Straight away I saw Aigerim, the fourteen year old girl with sad eyes. Photos of her feature prominently in the exhibition. She had travelled more than 340 km to be with us today and was accompanied by her sister and parents. As I had previously sent her (via Kamila) a CD player, I handed over four new pop CDs. She was really delighted.

Marat gave us a presentation featuring slides of Kimberley and me on previous visits to his hospital. He thanked us profusely for all our help and said that by raising the profile of his Oncology unit, the government had agreed to a significant expenditure in refurbishment and new facilities. He outlined the statistics for the incidence of cancers in Semipalatinsk and the Polygon and said it is still outrageously high, running at five times the national average.

He took us on a guided tour of the new breast cancer wing where we met patients in four person wards. In the first one, a young woman, recovering from surgery carried out only yesterday, was subdued and a bit bewildered by our presence. Kimberley held her hand and gave her some flowers.

In the next bed, a woman of 72 told us that she had been a teacher in the remote rural villages of the Polygon and had witnessed many nuclear explosions. Another elderly woman said that she had frequently been ordered to leave her home and stand in the street, holding her children by the hand, so

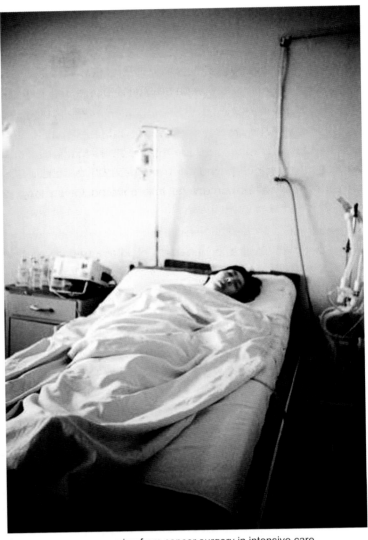

A young woman recovering from cancer surgery in intensive care,
Semipalatinsk

that she could witness the mushroom clouds rising in the distance. Now she had had a breast removed because of cancer. She was certain that this was as a direct result of the nuclear tests. We gave out little bundles of flowers to each of the patients and wished them a speedy return to full health.

Next Marat took us to a side-room where a large packing case, freshly delivered from America, lay unopened on the floor. Marat cut the binding tape and opened the box to reveal a mobile scanner purchased with my $25,000 donation. This was the piece of equipment he had coveted for so long, to enable him to go around the villages of the Polygon conducting tests on patients for suspected cancer.

The Oncology Centre is hundreds of kilometres away from most of the villages, served by roads which have been washed out or broken up for huge stretches, in weather conditions which veer from +40 in the summer to -40 in the winter. The ability to take a mobile unit to the people of the villages is therefore of vital importance. For me to see the tangible outcome of my donation unveiled and plugged in by a technician was awesome and quite moving.

Outside the hospital, Marat showed us a model of the intended total refurbishment of his hospital, which has now been agreed by the government and will be undertaken shortly. He said that without pressure from our campaign, none of this would have happened. He also thanked Erzhan Rackhmetov for his great support and efforts in getting funding agreed through the budget committee of the Majilis.

We met the Chief Doctor from the Children's Hospital in Semipalatinsk. He was looking a bit downcast, clearly

This mentally-handicapped woman displaying symptoms, all too common in the Polygon, due to radiation exposure

exhilarated at the good fortune which had overtaken his colleagues in the Oncology Hospital, but sad that none of this new-found largesse had come his way. He reminded me of the two occasions when we had visited his hospital and how we had expressed our great pleasure at the way the children were so well cared for and the wonderful staff. *"I have had no investment in my hospital and would really appreciate your help"* he said.

I realised that far from nearing completion, our work in Semipalatinsk was only just beginning. I promised him that the new focus of our campaign would be the Semipalatinsk Children's Hospital.

At 5.00pm we were chauffeured to the very grand Dostoevsky Museum to open the photo exhibition. This time the room was filled with hundreds of people. All the chairs were occupied and the aisles were packed solid with people standing and jostling for space. Once again the heat was oppressive. The Akim introduced each of us in glowing terms, the sweat running down his forehead and dripping off his nose and chin. After I spoke, Kimberley told the audience what she had said in Astana, calling for 25% of the investment there to be re-directed to the Polygon. This was met with huge cheers and applause. Obviously she had pressed all the right buttons as far as the people of Semipalatinsk were concerned.

At the reception following the powerpoint presentation, war veterans bedecked with medals, were lining up to speak to Kimberley and to be photographed with her. They each asked if they could kiss her on the cheek and then went off chuckling happily together! She had made their day.

Later we were taken to a private club where the Akim had prepared a dinner in our honour. Around 20 other guests had been invited. He presented me with a genuine leather-clad Kazakh shield and club and Kimberley with a beautiful painting of a Kazakh girl.

Then he stunned us all by saying that earlier that day he had telephoned the President to report that I had handed over a cheque for $25,000 to the Oncology Centre in Semipalatinsk. He produced a fax with a flourish. *"This has just arrived from the President"* he announced with some importance. *"In it, the President says that he remembers last September when he spoke to Mr Stevenson and, at Mr Stevenson's specific request, promised to match the $25,000 donation to the Oncology Centre. He has now fulfilled his promise. $25,000 will be transferred to the hospital".* Great applause met this news around the table.

Friday 22nd July 2005 – The Polygon

At 9.00am our convoy of vehicles arrived for the trip into the heart of the Polygon. The owner of several local goldmines, whom I had met on an earlier trip to Semipalatinsk, had given us the loan of three 4x4 vehicles and drivers for the duration of our visit to Semipalatinsk. Our gleaming, black Toyota Landcruiser and expert driver proved to be indispensable. Our driver knew the roads of the Polygon like the back of his hand. We took off at high speed in convoy and within a few kilometres of Semipalatinsk city the first major cracks and potholes appeared.

The roads across the steppe were built by the Soviets. They gouged huge trenches out of the desert on each side of the road, heaping up a bed of soil sometimes five metres high, topped off with a layer of asphalt. Where the extremes of hot and freezing weather had broken the road surface, hundreds of vehicles had carved a path along the sandy verges. Our driver would swerve off the broken asphalt and onto the thick, undulating gravel verge with great regularity, never slackening speed as we hurtled along the very edge of a five metre drop at speeds of over 80 mph. The groans and gasps from Elena and Kimberley simply made him smile.

Soon we arrived in the village of Znamenka. This was my third visit to Znamenka and we drove, as always, to the village clinic, where we set up the exhibition panels in the dusty main street and handed out European Parliament souvenirs to the villagers.

Beryk, the 26-year-old whose facial growth is reminiscent of John Merrick (the elephant man) came to see us once more, accompanied by his mother. As an otherwise healthy 26-year-old male, he now wants a girlfriend. In fact he has stopped taking the medication prescribed by his doctors to slow down the growth of his cancerous facial tumour, because he believes the doctors are trying to castrate him chemically.

Beryk grabbed Kimberley by the hand and asked what age she was. She said 32. *"She's too old for you, Beryk,"* I said and a tiny smile broke across his ravaged face, barely visible beneath the huge tumour.

I reminded the villagers that it was during my first visit to Znamenka in 1999 that the elders had said to me that they hoped I was not simply a 'disaster tourist'. They warned that they get plenty of these people who come to gloat at their

The barren steppe, Semipalatinsk

Struan setting up the exhibition in Znamenka, July 2005

107

suffering, cry crocodile tears, promise to help and are never heard from again. I said that I had been so moved by this warning that I had resolved to return as often as I could and to try to bring tangible help to these dignified and noble people. Immediately, one elderly man identified himself as the person who had spoken those words to me back in 1999. *"I remember clearly saying it to you"* he said, adding that he was delighted his words had had such an impact.

On to Sarzhal, where the local Akim and the Regional Akim were waiting at the roadside to welcome us to their village. Local girls in national costume were stirring a large basin of curdled mares' milk. Bright yellow lumps of fatty curdled cream swirled on the surface. Wooden bowls of this pungent liquid were handed to each of us and a tray of dried, soured mare's milk yoghurt was proffered. The acrid smell of these village delicacies sends an instant warning to the brain that the taste will echo their pungent odour.

For the unwary visitor there is no hiding place, however. Protocol demands that a sip of mares' milk and a nibble of dried yoghurt should be taken. The clawing, rancid flavour brings an immediate lump to the throat, but throwing up over the local Akim and his welcoming party would be frowned upon, so hard swallowing ensues, while welcome speeches are made through gritted teeth. Kimberley handed over one of our surviving bouquets to the Akim's wife earning instant brownie points and off we set for the village hall.

Again there were dozens of villagers gathered to greet us in the hall. The exhibition panels were hurriedly erected while we were led into a room packed with villagers, sweltering in +40

Kimberley and Beryk in Znamenka, July 2005

Kimberley sampling the local delicacy – curdled mares' milk in Sarzhal

degrees heat. The Regional Akim gave a long rambling introduction recounting our previous visits and the campaign we had fought to raise awareness of the victims of the Soviet nuclear tests in the Polygon. He said that when the people of East Kazakhstan had risen up in protest against the nuclear tests back in 1990 and had forced Gorbachev to call a halt, it was an action of great courage and of global significance. Later we learned that the Akim himself had just been diagnosed with a cancerous brain tumour at the age of only 42.

Next the chief village doctor gave her account of the continuing problems of cancers, chronic illness, disease and deformities caused by the legacy of radiation. She said that while services at the Oncology Centre in Semipalatinsk had greatly improved, there was still a need for better facilities in the villages. She said they really needed a pathology lab and clinic located somewhere in the middle of the Polygon, saving villagers from making the tortuous trip to the city which, because there is no public transport, can take many hours in each direction and in the winter is impossible because of deep snow.

The Akim invited some of the elders to make statements. One old gentleman, shouting vigorously but conducting himself like a seasoned public speaker, said that although our exhibition was entitled 'Crying Forever' we should not get the impression that the people of the Polygon were always unhappy. *"Twice in my life I've been happy"* he said. *"The first time was when the Soviets opened the nuclear testing site and the second time was when they closed it."*

He explained that in 1949 when Stalin announced that Semipalatinsk had been selected as the site for top secret military and scientific exercises developing new high tech weapons, the local population had been overjoyed at receiving such an honour. Little did they know the horrific consequences that awaited them. It was only following 607 nuclear explosions, many of them above ground, that the locals rose up in anger and demanded a halt to the tests which had brought cancer and misery to their people who had been cynically used as human guinea pigs.

After the meeting the Akim took us to his house for the usual village feast. A sheep had been slaughtered in our honour and the boiled head, complete with horns, ears and eyes, was served up to me on a plate as guest of honour. Knowing the custom from previous visits, I sliced off an ear and offered it on a fork to one of the TV journalists accompanying us, as the youngest person at the table. She looked as if this was a rather dubious honour to have befallen her! I then gouged out a white and withered eye and offered it to the Akim. Slices of meat had to be carved by me from the cheeks, nose and forehead and taken around the table to each of the guests before the meal and inevitable vodka toasts could begin.

Vast platters of boiled mutton arrived, interspersed with layers of white, blubbery fat which the Kazakhs forked into their mouths with gusto. Salvers heaped with fatty horsemeat followed, all washed down with overflowing bowls of curdled mares' milk. I picked gingerly at the plate of walnuts, which I knew came from Iran and the bananas, which are also imported. Virtually all local food, milk and water is still heavily irradiated.

It was time to leave. We still had another 150 km to drive across the steppe to our final village, Kainar, more than two

An angry village elder takes the floor in Sarzhal, July 2005

A woman tells her tale in Sarzhal, July 2005

hours away over the broken roads. Off we set in the searing heat and dust of the late afternoon and around 5.00pm saw the small, inevitable welcoming party parked at the roadside, awaiting our arrival. We were escorted into Kainar and taken to the village hall. Once again many locals had turned out to greet us and gazed in awe as the exhibition panels were erected, examining pictures of themselves, taken when we were last here in 2003.

In the large hall, we were ushered onto the stage by the Akim and I gave my usual introductory speech, followed by Kimberley and local MP – Erzhan Rakhmetov. When it came to the turn of the villagers to ask questions the sparks began to fly. It reminded us of the last occasion we were here.

The people of Kainar are highly articulate and never slow to grasp an opportunity to air their views. They were particularly aggrieved by the fact that although they had been promised a new water supply piped from clean, un-irradiated springs in the mountains, it had still not materialised. Instead the government was talking to them about a project to build a museum in the village. This infuriated them.

Once again Kimberley got great cheers of support for her suggestion to transfer some funding from Astana to the Polygon. Many had seen her saying this on their TV news and were right behind her sentiments.

Kimberley was taken outside to be re-united with the horse gifted to her by the Akim during our last visit in 2003. The elderly farmer who owned the horse told us that he had just returned from hospital where he was being treated for cancer. It seems no-one is free from the disease in the Polygon.

Different breeds of horses are reared for riding and eating in the Polygon

Kimberley rode the horse up and down the village street, to great applause from the villagers.

Hot and exhausted we were taken to the Akim's house for the final village banquet. The ubiquitous sheep's head was waiting for me at the head of the table, its teeth bared in a rictus grin. The toasts and pleasantries over, we set off home to Semipalatinsk, a journey of more than 350 km, which we almost completed without incident. It was actually within sight of the city lights that our driver slewed to a halt and announced that we had a puncture. The rest of the convoy quickly pulled up behind us and with a team effort, which would have brought a smile to the face of Michael Schumacher, changed the rear wheel in minutes by the dark and dusty roadside.

Saturday 23rd July 2005 – Semipalatinsk

Even on our final day in Semipalatinsk, the formalities continued until the last gasp. Escorted by a police car to the airport, a table had been set in the VIP lounge with breakfast including horsemeat and salmon caviar. Only Elena, our stalwart Siberian interpreter, could stomach a glass of Kazakh brandy at 8.30am!

Soon the old Yak-40 aircraft roared into view and parked outside the terminal building. We knew from previous experience that this ancient Soviet military 3-engined jet, offered an 'interesting' flying experience to say the least. Normally we would have been shuddering with fear, but after the flight in the Antonov 24, the Yak-40 held out the prospects of luxury travel by comparison. With only 36 metal seats, covered in thin cushions, it was built for operating from primitive airports in the world's severest conditions. It featured heavily during the Russian war in Afghanistan, but the few Yaks remaining in Kazakhstan when the Soviet empire collapsed in 1991 were left behind, deemed no longer airworthy! Two and a half hours later we landed in Almaty, happy to have survived yet another trip to the Polygon.

August 2005 – Brussels

Back in Europe it was time to take stock. We were still trying to arrange our photo exhibition in the US. A young Kazakh oil tycoon, Nurlan Kapparov, whose mother was born in Semipalatinsk has agreed to sponsor a major fund-raising dinner in New York city.

All of my focus is now on raising financial assistance for the Children's Hospital in Semipalatinsk. This superb institution is desperately in need of help. The caring staff show a degree of love and devotion to the babies and young children in their charge which is quite awe-inspiring. On each visit to the hospital I have never yet heard a child or even a baby cry.

However, the building is old and the equipment largely obsolete. A lot of help is required. Many of the children are orphans from the Polygon, their parents dead from cancer. Some are babies abandoned because of abject poverty. Others are born with terrible deformities and mental illnesses caused by the radiation which permeates everything. They need our help.

Many of these sick and orphaned children come from the Abay district of East Kazakhstan where a large number of nuclear tests were conducted by the Soviets. The Abay district is named after the great Kazakh poet and humanitarian Abay Kunanbaev. It was Abay who translated the works of Robert

Struan and Kimberley with a woman born deformed due to radiation, Sarzhal, July 2005

119

Burns and Robert Louis Stevenson into Kazakh. It seems to be the ultimate irony that Stalin should chose the home of this national icon who wrote about love and humanity, as the site of his nuclear tests.

Abay wrote *"If grief comes, resist, don't give up!"* His words must have given great courage to the people of Kazakhstan who rose up and challenged the might of the Soviet Empire, demanding a halt to the nuclear tests. For too long the nuclear testing programme in Semipalatinsk was a closely guarded secret. For more than 40 years the Soviet military authorities and the KGB kept their ugly secret hidden from the world.

It was my illustrious ancestor Robert Louis Stevenson who said – *"The cruellest lies are often told in silence."* But the people of Semipalatinsk refused to suffer in silence any longer. It was their bravery and their resistance in confronting the might of the USSR that brought this sickening episode to an end. Now it is the task of everyone to help rebuild this shattered landscape and to provide real help to these victims of the Cold War.

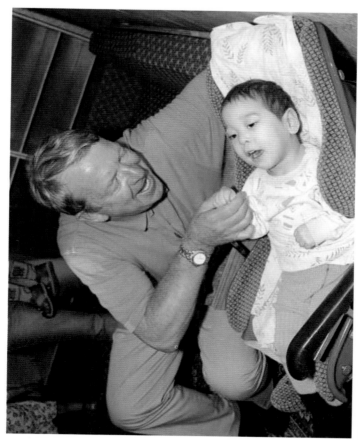

Struan meeting a severely handicapped girl in the orphanage in Semipalatinsk

Footnote:

Raising public awareness of the horror suffered by the people of East Kazakhstan at the hands of the Soviet Empire is the main objective of this publication and through raising awareness we hope to raise funds to help the Children's Hospital in Semipalatinsk. If you wish to make a donation, please send it to Mercy Corps Scotland at 17 Claremont Crescent, Edinburgh, EH7 4HX, Scotland, marked "Mercy Corps Semipalatinsk Fund".

The international series of photo exhibitions of Semipalatinsk was generously sponsored by:–

Unilever, Nike, Royal Mail, Lloyds TSB Scotland, Scottish & Newcastle, Diageo, The Republic of Kazakhstan, The European Commission and the EPP-ED Group in the European Parliament.

Struan with two youngsters in Znamenka
"I hope that the younger generation will enjoy a better future than their parents in the Polygon"